SURRENDER

A. A. KHAN

in conversation with

Shailaja Ganguly

YogiImpressions®

SURRENDER
First published in India in 2004 by
Yogi Impressions LLP
1711, Centre 1, World Trade Centre,
Cuffe Parade, Mumbai 400 005, India.
Website: www.yogiimpressions.com

First Edition, December 2004
Third Edition, July 2020

Cover photograph: Fawzan Husain
Courtesy: Mid-Day Publications

ISBN 978-93-82742-62-3

Printed at: Replika Press Pvt. Ltd.

Dedicated to the rank and file of policemen who work unceasingly, and without appreciation or compensation commensurate with their effort.

And, especially to the members of my ATS whose dedication and courage went far beyond their capacities in tackling armed and dangerous terrorists and gangsters.

CONTENTS

Foreword *vii*

Acknowledgements *ix*

Midnight's Ray of Light 1

From the Pen to the Gun 10

Living with Death 19

An Unholy War 31

A Classroom Called 'Life' 46

All in a Day's Work 58

On the Road to Perdition 66

My Gun and I 77

Yours Unfaithfully 82

A Rewarding Punishment 93

May the Force be with You 100

Mob Monstrosity 112

My God and I 120

Surrender 124

Endnote 136

FOREWORD

When the idea of this book took birth, Khansaab asked me what I thought and felt. It was a question which I could answer immediately. I stated bluntly what I had to say – perhaps taking a leaf out from his own unique style of functioning (which also got him into trouble occasionally).

I was pleasantly surprised to find that we instantly stood on common ground regarding what this book was *not*. It was not about knowing when, at what time, and in which district he was born, and recording all such biographical details of his life. It was not an ego-pampering exercise, gloating on past glories and feats. It *was* about sharing with the reader the key situations he faced in his career, how he handled them, his relationship with his team, the setbacks he faced, and the lessons life taught him as a policeman. It was about sharing his experiences, with the hope of providing invaluable pointers and lessons in the journey of our lives. It was about discovering the truth in Aldous Huxley's famous words: "Experience is not what happens to you; it is what you do with what happens to you."

Being associated with books primarily in the genre of self-development, I thought that in a book of this nature would lie a fascinating story. A story of a policeman whose job profile involved walking the tightrope of life over the precipice of death. What's more, Khansaab was notorious for not being an armchair warrior, and not sporting the bravery of being out of range! Needless to say, the book would, by default, have the tempo of an action-packed thriller, for he was known for his modus operandi of going right into the lion's den in order to capture the lion, as it were.

The task was to make the book relevant today, and always. There is a lot we all can learn from policemen. Most of us take it for granted that we will return home each evening from a day's work at the office, whereas in the policing profession such an assumption could well be a fatal fallacy. What's more, what would our levels of stress at work be, compared with those faced by policemen, especially when they are entangled in life-threatening situations, for the common good and not their own personal gain, and are not even adequately compensated while they're at it! Shrunyu Suzuki said that "life is like stepping onto a boat that is about to sail out to sea and sink," and this is perhaps amplified to a very high degree in the policing profession.

So walk with him and his team down alleys filled with terror, celebrate with them when they win their little victories, and be by their side when the chips are down. What this book will certainly do is make you be more thankful to God when you return home safe and sound every evening, to your family and loved ones. We also hope this book will make you spare a thought for the policeman, in whose shoes you are not.

Gautam Sachdeva
November 2004

ACKNOWLEDGEMENTS

Trite though it may sound, this book would not have been written but for the nagging insistence of my wife Mahjabeen, who has more faith in my abilities than I do. It would not have become a tangible reality without the persistence of my friend Gautam, who had the conviction to fashion it in the form of a book. It certainly would not have been coherent and readable without the writing skills of Shailaja, who gave sense and sanity to my ramblings, or Gregory, who did a fine job with the editing and final touches.

Perhaps the major motivating factor was my egoistical yearning to leave behind a memoir of my modest achievements which my sons Mansoor and Zaheer, my daughter Alisha, and my grandson Mikhail would read time and again, and remember me with affection and pride.

I am deeply indebted to my former Police Commissioners S. Ramamurthy and S. K. Bapat, whose leadership and guidance spurred me to perform feats beyond my calibre.

CHAPTER ONE

MIDNIGHT'S RAY OF LIGHT

I had just fallen asleep when the phone rang, strident, insistent. Pushing away the dense curtains of post-party grogginess, I switched on the bedside lamp and lifted the receiver. "Khan, is that you?" Even as I mumbled "Yes?" my mind sprang alive to say that this must be the voice of the newly appointed Police Commissioner of Mumbai. It was.

"Khan, intense rioting has broken out in Behrampada (a sensitive, strife-prone minority-dominated area of the city). The local police are finding it impossible to control the situation. Would you please go there? Now?"

Oh, no! my body screamed. After all, we had just wound up a night of revelry, to celebrate my promotion to the post of Inspector General, Maharashtra State Reserve Police Force. Obviously, this should have signalled the end of my nerve-racking twenty-hour 'days' as Additional Commissioner of Police, North Mumbai, and gifted me some time to loosen up a bit, to come to terms with this 'kick' upstairs (meaning, more of pushing files rather than rushing headlong into trouble-spots; but more of that later). Most of all, I was looking forward to a little leisure, some snappy tennis, some much-needed shut-eye... and now, this?

But of course, in a metropolis that never sleeps, a cop can almost never shed his uniform. Besides, as my rapidly-waking memory reminded me, I had given my word to the new commissioner that I would provide any assistance that he might need in order to slide smoothly into his tough harness, at least until the communal riots that had begun in December were over. Yet, I confess my slightly-befuddled brain did voice a weak *Why me?* There were at least four other officers of my rank who could have been sent instead, and let's face it – I had downed a few at my party. But, almost immediately, my rapid-action reflex came on – the reflex that becomes almost the second skin of every responsible individual caught in the crossfire of a demanding moment and unwilling limbs. "I'll be there," I heard myself say.

> *Life is something that happens when you can't get to sleep.*
>
> Fran Lebowitz

It was in the early hours of February 2, 1993. For over two months now, the simmering communal friction between the two major communities of this mega-city had been erupting sporadically. Just a couple of hours ago, I had felt relieved to think that I was off that uneasy saddle, that my portfolio would no longer include facing unruly mobs, using tear gas, or firing to disperse miscreants. Yet right now, I was hastily buttoning my uniform and rolling down the window to make the breeze clear the remaining mists in my head, as I tore across the city sitting beside the sub-inspector (who was my usual official escort) in his stripped jeep, while my band of five armed policemen sat behind, but facing outwards, as is the normal practice (a practice initiated by the British army while battling the IRA).

You see, it is much better to take the jeep's hood off and position your back-up men in this manner, because you then have a direct view of what is happening around you and can take swift retaliatory action – when a grenade is flung at you for example. Actually, I did not even have my own car that evening. But then, that's life – ever ready to spring a surprise when you least expect it. Keeps the adrenaline in peak flow, though!

When we reached the police station under whose jurisdiction this trouble-spot was, we found the deputy commissioner of the zone and his band of officers still trying to figure out how to curb the heated exchange of stones, burning rags, and missiles taking place between the inflamed residents of a Housing Board colony and the population of the shanty town spread out before them. Let me tell you, when a senior officer and his men choose to ask for reinforcements instead of jumping into the fray, it can mean two things – either they are scared to risk their own lives, or they do not have sufficient rapport, and therefore the courage, to interact directly with the citizens within their jurisdiction.

The local municipal corporator was also at the police station. He recognised and greeted me. "The crowd assembled within the slum colony is extremely hostile and agitated. They are feeling helpless because their opponents have an added advantage," he said. This was because the area they occupied was low-lying, whereas the angry mob, pelting them with its mindless fury, was operating from the terraces of the six and seven-storey high buildings that faced the slum.

Not wanting to waste a single moment, I asked, "Can we go in there and see what can be done?" "Yes, but you will have to come alone," was his unexpected reply. Now, I was familiar with this suburb, as it had been within my area of surveillance earlier. Besides, when the riots began, I was still in the hot-seat and on the move continuously, so I had a fair idea of the layout of the land too. Some of the by-lanes in there are actually narrower than the overflowing gutters around them. So there is no way you can zip through it in your secure vehicle. That is why, when a less adventurous officer hears that people are killing each other in a cramped quarter like this one, he often yields to the temptation to sit back, thinking, *Rather them than me*. For, once you step into the heartland of such areas, anything can happen – the local goons may surround, overpower and assault you without provocation. Frankly, it was an ugly place to be caught in a sticky situation like this one. I knew that too.

My earlier portfolio had helped me to understand the fabric of society in this riot-prone zone intimately, and some of them even knew me. Being prepared, or doing some homework in advance, always gives you an edge while playing tough games. My wireless had also given me enough information *en route,* on the potential gravity of the situation. Fully aware therefore, that a conventional strategy would never work in this hypersensitive zone, I had even begun formulating a quick plan of action. But, it was a plan that included my band of six officers. I had certainly not foreseen that I would be asked to go in there, alone!

Apparently, the frustrated residents had lost all faith in the ability of the 'saviours in uniform' to protect them. In fact, that was a major reason why the riots were so prolonged. Today too, their grouse seemed valid, because the terraces of the buildings from where the slum dwellers were being attacked had not yet been cleared by the police force. In fact, when the black gates of the makeshift shanty town finally loomed before us, we found that the residents had actually locked them from within to fortify themselves from the troublemakers outside, while someone had cut off the power supply. That again caught my preparedness on the wrong foot, for I was not carrying my flashlight. Life never thinks twice before posing awkward surprises....

Darkness and silence can either be embalming friends or sinister foes. It is all a matter of timing. Right now, the total blackout only served to multiply nameless fears and magnify the unease shrouding the entire area. On one side of those forbidding gates were terrace-loads of inflamed rioters, and on the other, random clutches of their enraged targets pooled together defensively with whatever weapon they could lay their hands upon – *lathis,* rods, hockey sticks, and the pet accessory of the rioter, the indigenous 'Molotov cocktail', fashioned by filling the odd bottle with petrol and inserting a wick. One simply could not let this go on. Without a second thought, accompanied only by the corporator and two of his men, I decided to go in to try and defuse the situation.

Have you ever got lost in a maze in the middle of a pitch-dark night, where the sound of your own footfall makes your heart leap? Where you can sense, but not see the red-hot anger brewing in the shadows surrounding you? I had patrolled through this mind-spinning web a number of times in daylight, but on that blacked-out night, if the local corporator and his men had suddenly abandoned me at any point in that tangled skein of narrow lanes, I know that I could not have found my way back.

So there I was, at 3 a.m. in this trouble-spot, trying to understand what provokes normal people (the collective consciousness, if I may call it so), to go berserk every now and then and invite prolonged misery upon themselves and their loved ones.

We have met the enemy, and it is us.

Walt Kelly

For the next hour and a half, I just walked in the torchlight provided by the corporator's two escorts, through those dark and deafeningly silent pathways, piecing together the jigsaw of helplessness, hostility, mistrust, protest and hatred, all simmering within those tense huddles of humanity. When I went towards the first group, half a dozen others joined me. *"Khansaab aa gaye"* ("Mr. Khan is here"), I heard someone whisper. The people had bunched together, to feel safer in numbers. They were angry, very angry, to begin with. Had I entered with my uniformed force, I am sure they would have pounced on us first, and then rushed into the buildings outside, igniting a major conflagration.

That is why I had agreed to go in without my men. Once you accept an assignment like this, you have to find a speedy way to dissolve the tension, ignoring any possible danger to yourself. So, firmly quashing the misgivings sprouting within, I deliberately kept my voice low and urged them to go home, to desist from taking the law into their own hands. I had to pacify their injured sentiments, assure them repeatedly that I would punish anyone who stoned them without provocation. As I mentioned earlier, this is a cramped colony where, most of the time, the built-up area happily eats into the street, so you just cannot navigate through it on wheels. The plus side of this coin being that when you move around on foot, you brush shoulders with the residents, you mingle, you have a finger on their pulse, you are right there, if and when a crisis occurs. Like now.

Perhaps that is why some of the locals who came forward to speak with me that night seemed to believe that I would give them a fair hearing. We knew most of the people there were ill-educated, and operated in the shadier walks of life with scant respect for the law. But that still did not justify a sudden onslaught on their homes and families.

Yes, of course, there are two sides to every coin, and communal rivalry is not an issue that can be solved overnight, because the wounds run deep and the scars take ever so long to heal. When dealing with a student or a labour riot, one has to keep the bigger picture, the long-term view in mind, because one does not want to antagonise these sections in the long run. But the situation is not the same when a no-holds-barred communal riot is on. At such times, all the formal training and procedures taught at police stations during riot drills just fly out the window! Try telling people bent upon slaughtering one another that an assembly of five or more persons is prohibited under Section 144!

At such trying moments the first method the police may opt for is a *lathi-charge*. When that fails to impact, tear gas is sprayed to disperse the unruly crowd. If the violence still continues unabated, that is when we pick out the leaders and fire, to hit only if we must, and then, only below the waist.

In every incident triggering off inter-communal violence, there is always one party that has the upper hand. I saw that here, the trump card was obviously in the hands of the attackers crowding the rooftops outside the slum. So if this carnage had to be arrested, *they* had to be stopped. Now.

The slum dwellers were pacified to some extent when I assured them that I would crack down on their attackers personally and agreed to halt retaliatory action.

As soon as I returned to the local police station, I sent a posse of policemen to clear out the terraces. Fast. Yes, the scuffle between the law-breaker and enforcer is part of the daily diet of every policeman on the beat, so some ugly scenes were inevitable, but finally, the troublemakers were rounded up, and by about 6.30 a.m., peace had been restored, at least for the time being. Of course, there was an outcry about the 'brutality' exercised by me (in apprehending persons armed with burning rags and stones, and missiles!), but that, as always, is part of the game. Both the opponents in every war, however big or small, are always convinced that *they* are the ones who are being wronged, right?

Any position that bestows upon you the mixed blessing of power over, and responsibility for a group of dissimilar people, is forever throwing up challenges like the one I faced that night. Situations when your world turns into a huge dormant volcano which can erupt with disastrous and far-reaching consequences, if your 'quick-think' does not help you take the right decision in the nick of time. What one needs (and I know I had) at moments like this, is total confidence in oneself, the firm conviction that one is fully equipped, both physically and mentally, to tackle the challenge thrown up by life. Fortunately, I have always felt like that, so I did not have to work towards major changes in personality to suit my job. Plus, having the ability to win the trust of the disturbed, often volatile people you are dealing with, definitely gives you a greater edge. Once you have succeeded in convincing any agitated group that you are on their side, they will automatically listen to you, quieten down, and give in to your request (not a command mind you!).

What also boosted my strength was the knowledge that, if the violence got further out of hand, I could have asked my men to intervene, act tough, and ensure compliance immediately. In any emergency, when your team hears you say, "I'm going ahead, follow me if necessary," it will never fail you; that's for sure. I had realised as I went up the ladder, that often, it is the lack of quality leadership that makes many an operation flounder. You will notice that a subordinate will always jump up to obey orders if he knows you are willing to share his peril, rather than trying to remote-control him while nursing a cup of tea!

I must warn you at this point however, that one must be on guard against one's confidence taking an upswing and turning into brashness, because that can spell trouble. This happens very often when you are the leader of the pack and feel you have an image to live up to. This headiness can even delude you into believing that you are infallible. Such notions can be lethal, especially in a profession like mine where you often deal with hardcore criminals or have to make hasty, un-premeditated moves in a crisis. For instance, I once actually ran over some hastily-flung wooden planks, to get across a distance of several metres between two high-rise terraces in order to nab some criminals. When a television crew wanted to reconstruct the scene for a shoot on the following day, I just could not repeat my 'stunt', because by then I had realised what a stupid and risky move I had made in the heat of the moment.

Again, a successful top gun in almost any field has to have a lot of tact and, in recent years, political contact as well. So if your sure-footedness comes into conflict with the wishes of your seniors or of politicians at a certain level, you are asking for problems. Like I did, at times. But then, all that mattered to me was my credibility with the public and my subordinates, period.

When we finally packed up, after that 'long day's night', it was almost 6.30 a.m. But the pink of the dawn streaking across the Mumbai sky was pale in comparison with the warm after-glow that suffused our hearts when we saw the relieved faces of the children, the old people, and all the bewildered residents of that slum colony. A major bloodbath had been averted, because prompt action had met the need of the hour. The positive force that works towards the good of the maximum number, had once again triumphed over the negativity that keeps surfacing in all walks of life. Like a constant challenge, it can pop-up anytime, anywhere, to tease you, test you, tempt you to drop your guard, lose your objectivity and composure, and yield to the pressure, the flaming impulse of the moment.

When this midnight drama had begun, I had been on a temporary high, thanks to my party, and had, honestly, felt cross and reluctant to shift from my cool and soft bed into the heat of action. But now, I knew I would not have liked it any other way.

CHAPTER TWO

FROM THE PEN TO THE GUN

Never, not even in my wildest dreams had I ever imagined that I would become a police officer. In fact, I wanted to be a writer. During those picnic years at college, where I was studying for my post-graduate degree in English Literature, I idolised my professor, devoured the classics, and eagerly experimented with the power of word-play. Each time I felt Shakespeare's immortal lines come alive through the rich baritone of my 'hero' in the lecture hall (my excellent professor), I was sure that I too would work for a doctorate on some aspect of modern English poetry and then go abroad to study some more, maybe teach as well, and of course, write!

I also loved interacting with all the 'everyday' people around me, like the little helper in the campus canteen, the man who ran a tiny tea stall in a by-lane, the shoeshine boy with an unforgettable smile, or the maid back home, who made sure my mauled wardrobe looked sane, yet again, before I returned. I was forever curious to find out where these human beings, who toil in the wings to provide us with so many essential services, draw their strength from. I wanted to know what makes their lives tick.

This heartfelt interest in the down-to-earth inhabitants of the 'real' world actually brought me my first earnings, when a just-born newspaper came to the campus looking for fledgling freelancers. Eager to have my say, I offered to interview some of my faceless friends so that at least some readers would be provoked into giving them a second glance. The publisher liked my idea (he must have also been delighted to have found someone who would fill up space, thrice a week, for a skimpy fee). So while I became a giddy-headed, part-time columnist, my professor became fully convinced that I had taken my first step towards becoming a man of letters.

What he and I did not know at the time, was that my mother had very, very different plans for me. Before I spill the beans on how she set them in motion, I must tell you that my mother was a very special person. Of course, every doting mother on earth is very special to her child. But what set my mother apart, was the amazing manner in which she could have her say and win her way through any opposition. For instance, once, some of my friends and I were threatened with suspension for trespassing into the girls' hostel and hoisting our shirts over the flagpole on its terrace. But suspension? Now that did not seem funny. Squirming a bit, I confessed my 'crime' to my mother (one could never, ever, approach my father with such an embarrassing story; he was way out of that orbit).

So what did my mother do? She dropped in on our college principal. She did not raise her voice. She did not make a scene. I have a suspicion that all she did was gently take him down memory lane to convince him that, at a certain hormone-intensive age, boys will be boys! End result? We got away with a few grunts from the Principal and a few whispered apologies from us, to convince him that the prank would not be repeated by us.

I think it was her impeccable upbringing that taught my mother the perfect strategy for playing to win. She came from a 'proper', *pukka sahib* background. Her grandfather had a title prefixing his name, her father was a judge at the Sessions Court, and so a certain confidence laced her carriage – a certain ability to achieve more with few words ran in her blood. I do not remember a single incident in my childhood when she flew off the handle while tackling the innumerable scrapes my seven siblings and I got into. But one thing I do remember. A mild reprimand from her was enough to get all of us red-faced and ready to bend backwards to please her.

Maybe those genes were responsible, much later, for putting the brakes on my mood-meter when as police chief, I had to deal with the *faux pas* of my boys in the force (or for that matter, with anyone who had already been roughed-up by circumstance). This is what past experience, one of the little tips stored in the memory bank of the subconscious, does for you. Indelible impressions of things you saw or heard, said or did, people, places, idols, demons – all lie in that Pandora's box, just waiting to receive a familiar signal and zoom into your present, sometimes to help, to teach you how to react (as they did, for me), at others, to hinder you from being who you are today.

Are you beginning to wonder how a daydreaming, novice writer ended up living the oftentimes nightmarish existence of a police officer? Well, why do you think I told you so much about my mother?

Yes, I admit that it was my mother – the only person I could never say "No" to – who decided that I should appear for the All India Services Examination. I had never disobeyed her; I never wanted to. But yes, I did wrestle within. I worked for the exam only half-heartedly, and yet, when the list of successful candidates was released, I could not believe my eyes. I had actually been selected! I think that made me realise for the first time, that there are some things in life which are beyond one's control. It is really as if there is an unseen master plan that chalks out your path, and at times, uses an agent to steer you in the right direction. In my case, that role was played by my mother.

As long as you struggle to free yourself from a circumstance or situation beyond your control, you resent where you are, you feel trapped, and you suffer. Your vision also stays warped, partial. On the other hand, if you accept what you cannot avoid gracefully, and clear your mind of all the 'I can't' and 'I won't' obstacles it has put up, you see a new road with fresh possibilities ahead. A spirit of adventure stirs your senses and you begin to look forward to playing a new, unexpected role... and yes, if you give it your all, you will be surprised at what life gives back in return. Of course it took me a while to work all this out, but once I had turned the corner of confusion and indecision and decided to give it a go, I actually perked up at the thought of a fulfilling, maybe even adventurous career in the public services.

Perhaps because I had observed the graciousness with which my mother always treated her hired help. Perhaps because I had inherited some of the awareness that while the rich can always bribe their way out of most situations, the poor have no one to turn to. A group of hooligans for instance, can terrorise an entire neighbourhood. A rat-pack of lewd eve-teasers can make life hell for a young girl walking alone on a deserted street, even more so if she comes from a less-privileged background and will hesitate to ring a doorbell to seek help. Whatever the root cause of this deeply ingrained concern, helping a weaker person, the image of being a guardian angel of the oppressed had always appealed to me. In fact, that is how I began writing my cub-reporter's column on ordinary people... and that is why, upon clearing the public services examination, I decided to opt for the police force. I must add that my greenhorn fancy was also enamoured of the awe the uniform inspires universally, and aware of the prestige and power that are part of the package.

Before this however, my only close encounter with a cop had taken place under highly forgettable circumstances. Two of my buddies from my college 'gang' and I were biking downhill at breakneck speed in a three-abreast-formation, with our arms around each other, when suddenly, this sub-inspector appeared out of nowhere. His threat that he would put us away for a couple of days and make our parents come to fetch us back, had literally jolted us out of our adolescence... and now, I was going to become a cop myself and play prefect in the classroom of life!

After I had made up my mind to give in to my mother and tap the in-built strengths she must have passed on to me, I did not look back at all at my punctured plans of aiming for the Pulitzer, except when I dropped in to say goodbye to my professor. He had always been a man of few words outside the classroom. "So you have decided to barter the possibility of becoming an outstanding writer for a few *salaams*, eh?" was all that he said, encapsulating the deep disappointment every sincere teacher must feel when he loses a promising student to what appears to be a less idealistic goal.

I could sense his hurt but I knew that he was only partially correct, because the world of creative writing is as manipulative, as ruthless as any other. There are so many who try so hard to reach the spotlight, so many who hog space centre stage without having what it takes, so many bright sparks who hang on to ill-paid jobs and then vanish without a trace. Besides, after really thinking hard, I had also realised that there was an 'action-man' in me who wanted me to do more than just write.

Today, I also feel that your final score in life does not depend so much upon which game you play, but upon how well you play it. The bouquets or brickbats do not count as much as your awareness, deep down, about how true you have been to yourself, how deftly you have handled the cards doled out to you by your birth and circumstance. During that uncomfortable moment in the college corridor, I was too raw to realise and tell him all this. However, the one thing I did know, even then, was that life had flung a new challenge at me and I had to put my best foot forward. I had to move on....

We are not permitted to choose the frame of our destiny. But what we put into it is ours.

Dag Hammarskjöld

After all those years of carefree sorties in the clouds of spiralling fancies, with a loving mother always there protectively in the background, starting over at the National Police Academy was like one hard landing. To begin with, I was the only candidate from my town. The 'groupies' who came from the same university, or had a godfather higher up in the police hierarchy, or could tap some political clout, swaggered around and even lorded over the harsh taskmasters, who drove the rest of us round the clock, through a tyrannical time-table.

Except for the occasional holiday with friends, this was the first time I was actually living away from my family, my home. In those painful days of initiation into a gruelling routine in an unfamiliar environment, I truly understood how it feels to be isolated, lonely, cut off. By the time I found a few other kindred souls swimming against the same tide however, I also managed to bandage my splintered self-esteem and stand up for myself.

Our days at the academy began at dawn with a full three-hour workout. The classroom sessions, though hectic, were not so taxing. But the 'physicals' took a heavy toll on those of us who had, before this, been just occasional sportsmen (that was my slot too!). Except for short breaks, we were on-the-go all through those two years of training at different centres. That was fine; it made real hardy boys of us all. What was not so fine was the fact that some of our trainers would act really mean at times. For instance, one of the physical training masters was a real sourpuss. He would call for any absent candidate, even if the poor guy was really sick, tell him he was a sissy, and then force him to run two rounds around the gigantic playground. Is this how a superior, anyone above you on the ladder, works out his own guilt or shame about personal inadequacies or shortcomings? By badgering someone within the stranglehold of his power?

I also got terribly miffed whenever I saw some of our stern trainers turning into fawning jellybeans when dealing with the lapses of class fellows who had VIP connections. This was my first hard look at some of the unfair games life plays at times. But I had opted for the world of the good, the bad, and the ugly with my eyes wide open. So I just bravely stuck my nose to the grindstone, more determined than ever to champion the cause of justice as soon as I got my first posting....

Have you ever been forced to bite off more than you can chew? I was, soon after my probation. I was appointed as the assistant superintendent in charge of one of the two sub-divisions of a fairly large district in Maharashtra. This was fine, because it was my maiden innings and I was raring to go. Within six months however, the officer in charge of the other sub-division had to move because of a domestic emergency. This unexpected development saw me getting a double responsibility – barely one step up the ladder, I found myself in sole charge of both the sub-divisions. My ascent did not end there, because soon, the superintendent himself took off on long leave, leaving 'pink-soled me' in charge of an entire district!

No, that did not make mere butterflies flutter; it made wild bats flap for a while in my belly. "Can I really deal with this just now?" I wondered. But not for too long. I did not panic and bolt. Instead, I decided to try and broaden my shoulders and carry this additional responsibility as best as I could. Therefore, when communal riots reared their ugly head during this tricky tenure and a replacement for the missing superintendent did not appear, I had no choice but to devise a strategy to quell them on my own. It seemed to work. For the riots subsided within the next two weeks... and I stayed in charge of the entire district for the next two months.

Except that now, I was additionally armed with the joyful awareness that I had managed to live up to the expectations of the higher-ups, who had not thought I was too young to handle this load. Panic can sometimes cloud your judgement and make you feel you are not capable of handling something new, something you had never bargained for. But if you keep that nervousness on hold, summon up some self-confidence and trust, and put your best foot forward, you may end up feeling as happily surprised as I did.

One more thing that caught me by surprise as I moved around incessantly in my open jeep on the dirt tracks that held this district together, was the fact that when you are on-the-job and eager to prove yourself, neither can the hottest sun give you a headache, nor can the swirling dust gift you an allergy. In such a short time, destiny had brought me out from under the cosy umbrella of a mother's love into the open challenge of having to face many an unforeseen event. Granted that truly loving your child means knowing when to hold close and also when to let go. But, had my mother actually realised what I was capable of, when she shepherded me into the selection exam hall? I have never asked her. But I have also never stopped being grateful for what she did.

The high that my short-term success brought me in those initial months was not without its share of lows, though. Take for instance, the day a minister came to my town to visit an industrial site where the labour union was staging a protest. Being in charge of the district at the time, I was present at the spot and suggested to the 'big man' that he should not get too close to the strikers. But, in an effusive move to flaunt his public relations skills no doubt, he suddenly walked up to the barricade. Some of the angry young men broke the cordon and he ended up *gheraoed* and furious.

As I have mentioned earlier, police code demands that we do not exercise excessive force, for a minor flouting of the law, upon protestors who are students or from the labour class. But obviously, one cannot expect a VIP, whose chair makes him think he is 'more equal' (bless George Orwell for that brilliant phrase), to understand this. Therefore, upon his return to base, he dashed off a nasty note to my superintendent who, in turn, pulled me up. He would, for I was already like a thorn in his side because of my unwillingness to play the servile understudy. What followed was a protracted battle of acrimonious letters that caused me a lot of unnecessary unrest, until I understood that one must not assert oneself too loudly before one's time. I also understood that everyone around you, seniors included, need not subscribe to your point of view – as long as you know that you are acting in accordance with your principles and the standards of objectivity or excellence that you have set for yourself.

On another occasion, when I was the Superintendent of Police in a district near Mumbai, I was accused of insubordination by a DIG (Deputy Inspector General of Police) because I protested about his move to dilute my authority. You see, it is the job of the superintendent to examine the dossiers and then allot postings to the inspectors and sub-inspectors within his district. Now this DIG, for some unknown reason, wanted to alter the postings given by me, thus overruling my authority. I was not one to take such unjust behaviour lying down, even if it came from an officer with a bigger tag. Of course, this also meant that I had to live through his attempts to malign me, just because I insisted that the rules of the game should apply to every player. But then, when you win some, you lose some. After all, the sunlight and the shadow have forever travelled hand in hand, haven't they?

CHAPTER THREE

LIVING WITH DEATH

Murder. The snatching away of another person's right to one more tomorrow. The shocking finale forced upon an unprepared target by the ugly hands of treachery. Unrepentant criminals, victimised women, ruthless terrorists, blameless bystanders. I have seen them all, lying stone-cold and inert, beyond defence, beyond judgement. With a vacant stare that triggers a flash of insight about the quicksilver span of life. Shrouded in silence that is a deafening reminder of the split-second chasm, the great divide between all that was and now... never can be. No, no matter how battle-hardened you are, you can never really get used to death. Especially not when it is murder and certainly not during your very first investigation.

I was at the club that evening, unwinding after a brisk game of tennis with the 'boss'. This was just before he bid good-bye to our district headquarters, leaving an inexperienced junior officer like me in sole charge for a while. Brushing shoulders with the top brass in the off-duty hour was the done thing in those days. But before I could take the collector on for our customary round of pre-dinner bridge, we received an urgent message on the wireless. Two unidentified dead bodies had been found in a culvert, barely ten kilometres from our district headquarters.

"Now that's a bloody good challenge, an unsolved crime in your very first innings. Here's your golden chance to test how well you can apply the balderdash you learn at training school on a real job, eh Khan?" smiled the police chief. I gave a firm nod, even as I fought down a rising tide of nervous anticipation. I went to the scene of the crime with grave apprehension.

It was not a pretty sight. The shaky light of the petromax lamp revealed maggots crawling over the partially decomposed flesh of a woman, maybe in her mid-thirties, and a small, seven or eight-year-old girl. The bright sari the sorry figure was draped in and the glittery frock the poor child was wearing may have led us astray, but for the shrewd observation of an older police inspector, who pointed out that the woman had brass bangles on her wrist. If she were from an affluent home, they would have been made of gold, he said, making me realise that you begin to see the bigger picture only when you learn to cultivate an eye for detail, only when you expand your vision to look beyond the obvious.

Identifying the woman seemed a daunting task, because there were no personal articles around, nothing to indicate who she was, or where she belonged. Her gaudy attire, cheap jewellery, and the fact that no one seemed to be looking for her and the little girl suggested that she was, perhaps, a sex worker. So wireless messages were sent out to police stations (based near the red-light areas) of towns in the entire district.

After two hours, we struck pay dirt. A message came from a nearby town that a sex worker with a girl child had indeed gone missing for a while now. After interrogating the women who knew her well, the unfortunate, oft-repeated story began to emerge. The killer had befriended the woman and lured her from her dubious lifestyle with the promise of marriage and respectability. Which young mother who is trapped in such an ugly cage with no hope of escape, ever, would not warm up to that? But the unfortunate victim was unaware that this was a replay of an old, old game, to con her of her precious nest-egg – the few items of jewellery that she must have collected painfully, over those scarred years, in the hope of giving her daughter a better life.

As soon as the dead woman's friends told us the name of the village her 'suitor' had come from, we knew we were on the right track, because it was very close to where the bodies had been found. Further investigations revealed that our wanted man was an inveterate gambler, who had abused his paramour's trust and used her ornaments to settle long-standing debts. Within twenty-four hours, the killer was picked up from a lodge. His father and brother testified that he had said he was bringing home a woman. But that was not enough to nab him. It was only after we recovered her jewellery, which he had sold in another town, that we could finally clamp the insensitive killer to a harsh sentence.

I had grown up in a home where compassion for the deprived was ingrained in us, where we were taught to extend a helping hand towards those incapable of defending themselves. So it did not matter that the unwanted woman and her hapless child had no one to miss them or mourn for them. What mattered was that cold-blooded crime had to be paid for, that justice had to be done.

Taking up this maiden challenge and solving the crime within just a day and a half, and wrapping it up totally within seventy-two hours, thanks to the whole-hearted cooperation of my astute officers, also brought home another truth – that I did seem to have an aptitude for this profession; that I had chosen right. True, on this road, I would be constantly courting death or seeing its many faces, as I had just done. But that was okay by me, in fact, it was much, much better than choosing the wrong profession and settling down to a dull and vapid existence.

Soon there was another case of multiple murders in the same district. In this case, the victims were a woman and her two children. A probe revealed that the killer was a furious fifteen-year-old stepson to whom the new mother had been very cruel. She would lie about his supposed 'misdeeds' to the father, who was so besotted with his young second wife that he would batter the boy with whatever he could lay his hands upon. This was a gruesome version of life imitating art (remember all those fairy tales peppered with nasty step-moms?).

One day the wily woman went too far. She threatened to tell her husband that his "oaf of a son" had tried to molest her, not realising that there is no weapon as deadly as wounded self-esteem. In horrifying retort, the boy hacked this deceitful usurper of his dead mother's 'empire' and sadly her two babies too, with an axe. He then buried the weapon and disappeared. When we nabbed him he was quick to confess, but stayed convinced that he had only done the needful.

Society prepares the crime; the criminal commits it.

Buckle

This is how unconventional and immediate tribal law is. Killing is not of as much consequence as being stripped of your honour, your self-respect, or your rightful place in society. A trivial quarrel, a minor fracas over money matters, and of course, a tiny slight or insult are reasonable cause for murder. A similarly outraged person in an urban setting is a little more conscious, a little more fearful of the law. Apart from gang killings, which operate on a different system of justice altogether, urban murders are generally the result of quarrels over large sums of money or property. 'Heart trouble' (caused by a rebuff, betrayal, an extra-marital affair) is another common motive. Except in the shanty towns, which spring up on the fringes of urban civilisation and continue to practise 'homegrown' methods of dispensing justice. In those overcrowded slums, even a dispute over a common water tap can lead to an untimely death.

It is not too difficult to understand the inside story, the murky mindscape of a murderer obsessed with revenge. His impulsive crime is generally the sorry fall-out of unchecked anger, following the loss of face, money, property, a paramour. It is the frenzied move of a baseline individual who does not reflect before reacting, who is ensnared within the web of his own brute logic. But physical assault, torture, and almost gleeful murder that is prompted by gargantuan greed alone? Now that is a much more gruesome story....

Take, for example, the case of an incredibly cool criminal called

Tony, whose penchant for living rich was paid for by so many innocent lives. Tony was a strapping body builder with not a spare milligram of excess fat on his sleek limbs. He was also a Taekwondo expert, who only frequented the health clubs at five-star hotels. He loved life in the fast lane. He also loved to raid jewellery shops at off-peak hours and decamp with the booty, often leaving behind a 'silenced' salesman who would tell no tales, not now, not ever!

Although his strikes covered several cities, the man could not be caught because he did his homework well and never left a single clue behind. His was a classic example of a super-intelligence gone wrong. Tony was a manic genius who, with meticulous planning and flawless strategy, always played to win. What was tragic was that the goal of this extraordinary brain was unabashed material gain, and he had absolutely no qualms about torturing or doing away with anyone who came in his way.

Patience is the name of the virtue needed in abundance when you deal with an offender who can foresee your every move. You have to keep your chin up. You have to keep trying to induce the wrongdoer to make that one false move that will give you an edge and tilt the scales in favour of justice and truth. So we kept probing, speculating, watching, planning, till one day, out of the blue, an informer called. He was the envious, 'have-not' relative of one of the jewellers who had been robbed. And he knew how to get in touch with Tony. Perhaps that is how Tony identified his targets – through disgruntled insiders.

In a world ruled by double-dealing and counter-espionage, this is not unusual. The shrewd 'accomplice' had probably got a cut from Tony's haul at his relative's store and was now prospecting further, for a cash reward from us in return for valuable information about this wanted guy. So we put our heads together at the police headquarters, cashed in on Tony's weakness for diamonds, and laid a trap....

Posing as a dealer in exceptional stones, one of our inspectors contacted this slippery sadist and fixed a meeting. The venue was one of the empty flats at our disposal, used for clandestine meetings like this one. Planning to eliminate the dealer and whisk away the rocks, Tony came equipped, but was soon overpowered by the strong arm of the law. The five-year prison term may have slowed down his pace and saved a few more unsuspecting staffers in jewellery shops, but it did nothing to reform Tony's warped mind.

After his release, Tony graduated from thieving to gangsterism, still hungering for the big bucks and luxuries he did not want to earn rightfully through physical or intellectual labour. He could have harnessed his fitness fetish and smart looks to earn big bucks as a star trainer, for goodness' sake! But no, Tony was a man in a big hurry; he wanted too much, too soon, and in any which way, at that. So he wrote his destiny accordingly and threw it all away – his skills, his chances, his dreams and finally, his very life. His death in a police encounter in 2002 may have unleashed more relief than grief, but it is a definite pointer to the downhill road reserved for intelligence abused. When you sow a wind, you have to be ready to reap a whirlwind.

Also thronging this slide to self-destruction are the 'hit-men' – those robotic terminators, all wired to kill. At times, for no more than a few thousand rupees, which they may never see if the operation boomerangs. Paid puppets of the big players like builders, land sharks and local dons, these young men are often the debris thrown up by socio-economic upheavals, forced by unhappy circumstance to take to the life of crime.

The indefinite textile strike of the 1980s in Mumbai provides a classic example to show the traumatic consequences of investing trust in a short-sighted labour union leader. Thousands of shop-floor workers bartered the simple joys of a regular income and a modest nest to return to, for prolonged misery that made mockery of their hopes and criminal 'hirelings' of their devastated children. Deprived of regular meals, education, and the right to dream of a better tomorrow, many youngsters fell prey to the promise of quick money held out by the henchmen of local goons.

Adding fuel to the potent mix of deprivation, ignorance, and hopelessness was the glamourous villain, the 'bad guy' of the Indian cinema. This undesirable but larger-than-life role model was a crucial part of their lives, because he was the only entertainment their slender pockets could afford. Watching this gun-toting dandy zooming around on fancy wheels, or living it up in a world lush with wealth, wine, and women, week after week, made it that much easier to walk away from a bitter and broken reality into the snare of an underworld group.

Whether the underground 'training school' has been founded on a small-timer's strategy for personal gain or it is part of a larger religious crusade thought up by a brilliant fanatic, its 'syllabus' remains the same. And the rewards? Juicy carrots, if you 'execute' your orders well and ask no questions. Obviously, such an abnormal routine slowly, slyly, but surely distorts your outlook and systematically destroys finer values. The 'guides' either underplay, or glorify, the ugly fate that awaits you if you make one wrong move. Just like those movies, which project the hi-jinks and sexploits of the villain in many more frames than those capturing his fall – a fall that slaps reality back on the screen and more often than not, abruptly cuts short the role of one more lost soul.

That was the fate that ultimately befell Tanya, a sharp-shooter attached to a well-known don of Mumbai. Tanya hit the headlines yet again, when he shot at a moving target in broad daylight in a busy suburb (also killing two harmless hawkers who came in the way), before he blithely sped away. With the nonchalance that becomes an integral part of a brainwashed *bozo* who does not, cannot "make reply or reason why". For, unlike the honourable warriors of Tennyson's Light Brigade, he and his ilk forever remain shunned outlaws, whose do-or-die missions are just mindless transactions, undertaken only to earn 'a few rupees more'. Tanya's heinous act unleashed panic and insecurity among the local residents and we decided to ferret him out from the gang's hidey-hole in the heart of the city.

Originally housing the mill workers' families, this gangland stronghold was a virtual warren of closely spaced tenements fortified by a twenty-foot wall with a huge iron gate. Manage to get past that outpost and you reached a smaller one, through which entry was possible only in single file. This gate had a small shrine adjoining it. The ringing of the innocuous bell in this temple was echoed by a bigger bell in another temple within the 'fort'. This served as a smoke signal to the inmates that there were trespassers at large.

To achieve success in any demanding assignment you have to keep your wits about you, boost your back-up forces, and do your homework well. Our plus points in this daring raid on a dreaded don's hideout were: we had a reliable informer who had been with the gang and had lived in this 'maze' earlier, we had dozens of private cars with plainclothesmen on the job, and we had surrounded the place from all sides. But even a few choice opening moves do not guarantee a checkmate, particularly in such deadly matches and especially when you are sparring with grandmasters of the con-game. Your plan has to be fool-proof, your stance absolutely vigilant, and your morale – indefatigable!

We had scheduled our raid to coincide with the 'problem hour' at this don-land. We were told that everyday, between two and three in the afternoon, either the big man or his co-pilot held an open-house here to solve money disputes through speedy 'out-of-court' settlements in which a few lakhs exchanged hands (obviously in quick response to prior phone calls made by the don's diabolic network). Since we knew beforehand that the smaller gate was kept partially open at this time, it was easier for my boys to overpower the guards and barge in with the SRP (State Reserve Police), who had been in touch on walkie-talkies, following close on their heels.

Outside, our informer sat in a police jeep, willing to help, but wearing a *burqa* to avoid any nasty retaliation from the devotees of the demi-gods within the sanctum. Our trucks, jeeps, and cars had virtually flooded the area, leaving no gap for anyone to escape. Even the ACP (Assistant Commissioner of Police) of that area and his staff were there. But when we stormed in and ransacked the quarters, checked every *chawl*, every room, we found no one. Not a sign of the offender or any of his cronies.

The local police gloated (a cheap victory over a higher-up on the ladder never fails to bring out the claws, does it?). *We had already raided this place last night. We could have told you the birds have already flown, if only you had asked us*, their collective smirk said. My heart dipped momentarily. This was a massive operation. There were a couple of hundred men swarming the place, besides reporters and television crews. Had all our meticulous calculations been a colossal waste of time and effort? Were we to turn back with egg on our faces?

No, giving up at this point was like playing right into the hands of this self-styled hero, who would automatically notch up a bonus point for himself in the eyes of his cronies and the general public. It was time therefore, to do some soul-searching, to find out whether we had explored all the loopholes, to find out whether we had really done enough. No, we could not return without making one more attempt to smoke out our quarry. If you can calm an agitated mind and then recharge it to 'quick-think', it becomes your best friend once again. Like mine did at that moment. For I suddenly realised that now was the time to use our trump card. Now was the time to put some more pressure on our informer – to force him into total recall, to make him remember if there was anything he had overlooked, to find out, once more, whether there was anywhere else to look.

The move paid off. The man recollected that there was a basement with bunkers for the 'big boys', where he too had lived in hiding for a while. But he was too scared to emerge from the vehicle and show us the location. Never mind that. The valuable information was enough to inject fresh fire into our search and make us turn the place upside down, one last time. Again, we drew a blank. Nothing, no one. But this time my pulse would not slow down; this time I could hear my inner voice grow louder, and so I kept prodding my men to keep going, to keep searching.

Our 'weapon' was the crude, native *dhumas,* an iron rod with a flat head. By tapping it on the floor one could sense if there was a built-up level below. Like night-watchmen we pounded our way through two *chawls,* but in vain. Finally, we reached the third one. Each of the flatlets in the *chawl* comprised a living room, a toilet, and a tiny kitchenette with a *mori* (drain) in a corner. It was in one of these that the *dhumas* made a tell-tale, hollow sound. I looked around the sparsely furnished, cramped accommodation and suddenly spied this big drum of water stored under a dry tap. Something told me to drain the water and shift the drum... and sure enough – under it was a narrow hole, hardly two feet in diameter. This led to a tiny, airless, six-foot by six-foot square bunker, where our cunning catch – the terrible Tanya – lay crouched along with his understudy and our biggest haul, to date, of arms, explosives, and ammunition. By not walking away at that last hopeless moment, we had done it! We had got our wanted guy.

Imagine being escorted by a motorcade of thirty-odd police vehicles through a sea of ten to fifteen thousand people. With sirens announcing your arrival at every traffic signal; with armed guards poised to prevent any counter-attack to rescue you from the clinging embrace of the law. Yes, in a macabre procession, this cold-blooded killer had a historic journey from the claustrophobic basement he was holed up in, to my office, where he would answer questions. Many questions....

"I will talk only to Saab (meaning me)," Tanya said. Probably because he had realised that even in the heat of the moment of capture, when my exhausted, foggy eyes had suddenly lighted upon him crouched in the black hole, I had not pulled the trigger.

The interrogation began and the ugly details began to spill out. Among the multiple crimes that had led to this arrest, Tanya had shot at a financier for a big-time, rival don. Since the man was in a car at the time, the wild spray of bullets had killed the two hawkers as well. Tanya seemed totally unmoved by this sad fact. Once you enrol in a violent game, a 'hit' or a 'miss' is all part of it, his blank demeanour said, as he coolly reeled off a shocking list of previous conquests and then rounded off with a chilling, "That should do for now. Tell me, how much can a man remember?"

His accomplice, who was also caught, confessed that he had been with Tanya during five hits but had accomplished "only two" on his own so far. As Tanya's was a non-bailable case, he was sent to the Yerwada Jail (India's Alcatraz, swarming with some of the most vicious minds and bloodied hands in the country). That should have been the end of his chapter in my life. But believe it or not, he actually sent me some scribbles now and then, from his prison cell. They would contain titbits about some of the plotting and planning that went on there among captive fugitives whose twisted minds are still closed to reform, who will never say die.

However compelling the reasons why he took to a criminal way of life, the indelible fact is that Tanya was a cold-blooded murderer who killed for money and not for any form of redressal of justice. When you have anaesthetised your finer feelings forever and are able to indulge in mindless violence repeatedly, a perpetual offender is what you are. So there was no question, whatsoever, of feeling any sympathy for him.

But what prompted Tanya to send me those notes, to stay connected with his captor? Was it the fact that I had desisted from snuffing out his right to tell his side of the story, with one more 'encounter death'? Was he trying to win me over, and thereby get off with a lighter sentence? Or was it the faint voice of a long-buried boy, who had wanted to make his mark in a big, bad world, but having lost his way, ended up being a marked man instead? I will never know.

Nor is there any law more just, than that he who has plotted death shall perish by his own plot.

Ovid

What I do know is that two years later, when Tanya was killed by a rival gang member, *en route* to his trial and in spite of being under police escort, I realised yet again, that there is no getting away. Like the proverbial tortoise, justice has a way of catching up with you, sooner or later. Even if it is administered by jungle law, as it happened with Tanya. As for the stars favouring me on the day of his capture, all I can say is, yes, good luck does happen, but only when opportunity meets preparedness.

CHAPTER FOUR

AN UNHOLY WAR

You need someone who believes in you. Especially when the night grows longer and the road ahead seems endless. At such glum moments, it is only by the steady light of another person's faith in you that you can find your way out of that tunnel of self-doubt and into the sublime sunshine of renewed confidence.

When I took over as the Additional Commissioner of Police (North) in Mumbai (in 1990), I found myself staring at a city file, reeling under a pile of unsolved crimes – robbery, abduction, murder... each more horrifying than the other and none appearing to be the handiwork of fly-by-night, one-time offenders. A couple gunned down brutally in their own home, only because the man had married a Sikh girl. An entire family of five, which included three innocent children, abducted and then deliberately mowed to death (for God's sake!), under a brute's truck-wheels, in the wilderness framing the city's outskirts. Here too, the girl was a Sikh who had married outside the community. Another extortion target (who was an inter-state transporter of goods, and from the same minority community) was felled by a bullet. A bullet that first ripped through a door and then through his defenceless skull, before embedding itself in a steel cupboard.

If men are so wicked with religion, what would they be without it?

Benjamin Franklin

Upon careful scrutiny over the next few days, I began to see the thread running through these blood-curdling killings and sensed a chilling aura of desperation. Desperation coupled with access to deadly, automatic weapons. Desperation and the need for a lot of money to fuel some twisted mission. But most of all, desperation to unleash a wave of terror on the hardworking and peaceful Sikh community of the city.

Now, the major disadvantage I faced in policing this metropolis, was the fact that each of the widely spread out police stations here dealt with the offences committed within its area of jurisdiction on its own. There was no common forum where everyone in the force could be made aware of how many, or what kinds of criminals were at loggerheads with the law. It was this weak link, this minimal coordination and exchange of information among the city's protectors, this lack of a united front, so to speak, that became fertile ground for a big-time striker to spring forth now and then, knock down his next quarry, and immediately melt away into the shadows of a distant suburb, till it was 'harvest-time' again.

Another big hurdle that blocks any form of troubleshooting for anyone, anywhere, is not knowing where the seed of the widespread malaise lies hidden. In my case, the problem lay in trying to read the mental map of an unknown gang-leader who was able to kill without remorse. To prevent 'outsiders' from 'defiling' the believers in his community, his group seemed to have embarked upon a crusade of sorts, however mixed-up the values that inspired them and however bloody the trail they left behind. What was their cause? How could we locate them, break them, or pin them down?

If you are the head of any working unit, big or small; if you are the one who plans, delegates and initiates action, the one who shoulders the overall responsibility, but does not apportion the blame, you will know exactly how I felt at the time. Like I said, locating the root cause of a problem that is growing bigger by the day can temporarily frustrate you, rent your confidence, dim your fire. But, if you manage to hang in there till the first glimmer of reasoning dawns, then the ball is in your court once more, and you have just earned the right to belt out a tight serve that can knock the wind out of the sails of any opponent. An opponent who may even be caught napping, because he has turned a trifle over-confident and complacent because of your earlier goof-ups and his past record of easy victories.

When the initial pieces of any giant jigsaw begin to fit into each other smoothly, the eagerness to accelerate action sharpens. After many hours of brainstorming, we deduced that all these 'unholy' crimes clearly pointed at a team of terrorists from Punjab who had escaped to Mumbai after the local police began a crackdown. They wanted to make some quick money through extortion from their local 'brethren' to fuel their dream of a separate state for their religious minority. The gang was led by a mastermind whose fanaticism and consequent unreason was creating shock waves in the city.

Extremists think "communication" means agreeing with them.

Leo Rosten

As soon as we arrived at this conclusion, I felt the urgent need to launch a systematic counter-attack. Obviously, the existing strategy was not working. So I wanted to assemble a special force, drawn from all the police stations that had been stumped by these sharpshooters' deadly games. The hand-picked team would have earnest officers recommended by their respective stations. Each would be between twenty-five and forty years of age. Besides being reasonably fit, they would have proven skills in interrogation. In addition, they would be boys who had cultivated a good network of informers over the years. You must know that this infrastructure is an invaluable asset of every on-the-job 'police-hound'.

Just as I was putting the final touches to this proposal, the enemy struck again. This time, in broad daylight, at a busy traffic junction manned by a sub-inspector and two policemen. A jeep carrying heavily armed men jumped the red light. The officer chased it on his motorbike. On getting closer, he realised that the passengers were carrying automatic weapons. This made him take a sharp U-turn and hop off at the nearest call-box to inform the Police Control Tower (based at the headquarters) about the suspicious-looking vehicle. What the poor man did not know however, was that this was going to be his last conversation on earth. For, just like in those B-grade, pulse-jerker movies, the miscreants had reversed too. They then sidled up to the phone booth, and even as the unsuspecting officer was talking, pumped bullets into his back.

The carnage did not end there. They also chased the two policemen, who were by now running for cover, and shot them dead as well. At 11 a.m. on a bright and cloudless day. In full view of over a hundred dazed pedestrians at a teeming crossroad. This was the last straw. It put my back up. It made me swear I would get them. It made me rush to the commissioner with my proposal. The time to retaliate was NOW!

However brilliant or far-sighted you may be, if you are not the 'number one' on the ladder in any organisation, you cannot take policy decisions on your own. You need the go-ahead of the person at the helm. You need a supportive leader who knows your potential and will not breathe down your back. I was most fortunate to be answerable to a man of few questions. A man whose ego did not totter because a subordinate had tossed up a better idea. Perhaps that is why my superior – the Police Commissioner of Mumbai – gave me the green signal to create that Anti-Terrorist Squad (ATS). The battle to squash separatist forces trying to undermine a nation's unity, the battle against a misconstrued faith that paints its history in blood, the battle for justice that is universal... that battle was on!

As soon as my proposal was okayed, the actual search for my iron men began. I looked hard for youthfulness, zeal, tenacity, a high threshold in handling stress, and above all, a noteworthy record of personal courage. This last qualification was an absolute must, because every operation of the squad would be a high-risk mission.

A cornered terrorist is at his most dangerous. When dealing with such desperados who have nothing to lose, death is like a constant companion. That is because the chances of getting caught in the crossfire are high – in fact, too high to be overlooked. So I just could not afford to recruit teammates who would crumple at a crucial moment, who would panic in an emergency. This is how the ATS was born.

Knowing that the boss was on our side added zip to our investigations. We reopened all old cases which had the scent of terrorist activity, dug out all the suspected associates, and began massive interrogations.

For a month and a half nothing worked, nothing came up. No pointers, no clues. This was a trying period. A period spent praying for a breakthrough and at the same time devising strategies to boost the morale of our brand new team. We constantly put our heads together, conducted many a mock operation, ate makeshift meals, shared problems and jokes, in short, did our best to keep the heat on. Then, on a bright January morning, as I was sweating my blues out on the badminton court, my ACP called!

"We have managed to break down one fellow," was all he said. My heart soared and I rushed to the police station, where the boys had been questioning a few suspects. In that artificially-lit basement cell, I saw the first ray of hope. It seemed as if we would beat these bulldozers, who were so brazenly challenging our authority, yet! Our captive was huge, almost six-feet-four-inches tall, with a resilience to match. But our persistence wore him down, till suddenly, his defences caved in, and out poured a volley of prized information. There were eight members in this terrorist group (of which three had been trained in a neighbouring country), he said. He also promised to lead us to their hideout in a smaller town of a neighbouring state (Baroda, in the State of Gujarat). At long last we had a valuable lead, thanks to the unrelenting effort put in by my boys over the past few weeks. I came away from that interrogation with a renewed burst of energy and a lighter heart.

Believe it or not, the hot-blooded hulk who gave us this major tip-off actually metamorphosed into a pet informant. Only my boys knew his identity, and even they referred to him only as *Popat*, the Hindi word for parrot. Who says men under duress lack a sense of humour? Why did this man spill the beans to begin with, or stay on thereafter, to become an invisible friend? Was it because the hard grilling had managed to penetrate through the gray clouds of his misplaced ideology? Maybe, maybe not. The fact remains however, that but for his loosened tongue, the trail would have turned cold. Bringing home the truth that one way or the other, we are all inter-connected and inter-dependent. The faster we realise this, the easier it becomes to pool in complementary skills and work towards goals that generate the greatest good for the largest number. What Martin Luther King, Jr., in that masterpiece of a letter protesting against the inhuman segregation of the blacks, described as the "inescapable network of mutuality".

According to *Popat*, who regularly transported truckloads of goods between Punjab and Mumbai, he had met the terrorists when he stopped for fuel in Baroda. He offered to take us to their hidey-hole. This was hot information. There was not a second to be wasted. We had to rush there and nab them before they escaped once more. I dialed the commissioner. He could have asked for a breather to work out the details. The request would have been justified, because the offenders now came under the jurisdiction of the law-keepers of another state. But thankfully, this man was not one to let the grass grow under his feet in an emergency. All he said was, "Are you confident of handling this?" "Yes," I replied, and that was enough.

My officers left for Baroda that very night in eight private cars, while the arms followed in a police jeep. But we gave the rest of the force an impression that we were going by train. This was essential to cover our tracks and prevent sabotage. As soon as the squad reached Baroda, the boys just dumped their belongings in a hotel and rushed with *Popat* to the peaceful housing colony, which knew nothing about the deadly trespassers it was shielding. We had contacted the local police for a supplementary back-up force, to enable us to completely surround the bungalow where our 'wanteds' were holed up. Tension mounted, the minutes crawled by....

Suddenly, one of the boys saw a man coming out of the bungalow. "That is Baldev Singh, the leader of the group," *Popat* whispered. But no shot was fired. We let him go. That was because we wanted to capture everyone within that house at the same time. We did not know how many more of these hardcore heavyweights were still in there, and we did not want even a single one to get away scot-free after the panic they had let loose, the heartbreak they had caused to so many of their blameless victims' loved ones back in Mumbai.

It is only when you harness both knowledge and prudence, that you can reap the best result in any endeavour. Having cornered our villain, we knew that we would get our chance to strike. But just now, it was time to lie low (literally, as we were vulnerable out there in the open space facing the bungalow). It was time to wait....

Our chance to strike arrived at about 9 p.m., after Baldev returned. First, the tyres of the car in which he had returned were deflated to prevent escape. An early victory came when one of Baldev's men came out with his wife and child (perhaps upon some suspicion), and was apprehended within five hundred metres of the building. After this, one of our officers picked up the loud hailer and challenged the inmates, asking them to surrender. Immediately, all the lights inside went out. A grenade flew towards us and exploded, but no one was injured. This was followed by a hailstorm of bullets to which our team retorted with equal anger. We kept repeating our warning that they were completely surrounded and should lay down arms, but when reasoning is blindfolded by rage, all that you say just falls on deaf ears.

In this 'open' battle, our only cover was a few sand-bags. Besides, my boys were mainly policemen from the force with no specialised skill in commando warfare. However, as the bullets flew around us in that do-or-die moment, I am proud to say that this handicap was overpowered by their exemplary courage and intense resolve to triumph over the dire situation. So they kept their chins up and retaliated for eight stormy hours. Some of them had to get really close to the house to blow out the windows. And they did just that. They were virtually unstoppable on that memorable night.

But then, Baldev was equally adamant. Do you know what his climactic move was? He went up to the terrace, and actually jumped across a distance of several feet onto the rooftop of the adjoining building, in total darkness! After which, he began to slide down a drainpipe in a last attempt to get away, a final effort at one-upmanship. But my team spotted him. A shot rang out... and the curtain came down on the life of a driven man. A man who obviously had a shrewd mind, plus the ability to manage both a group, and an agenda. A man with tons of brash courage and a diabolic will that would brook no opposition. He could have been a man of substance in the 'real' world, but for the walls in his fundamentalist mind. Walls that cramped and minimised his vision. Making extortion seem proper, turning ugly murders into glorified sacrifices for a divine cause. Yes, I do believe that daredevils like Baldev are born with 'a right to be remembered'. Except for a twist in the tale that makes them choose the wrong road and worse means, thereby earning notoriety in place of fame.

Seven men and two women (Baldev's wife and old mother) came out of the hideout and surrendered to us that night. The wife swore that there was no one else in there, except for her child. She wanted to go in and get it. This aroused our suspicion. We were now sure there was more of the group in hiding. So we inched forward, and sure enough, the two terrorists who were still inside started throwing grenades at us. We had called for heavier weaponry from the local armed police. We now used this to blast the grills and windows of the house, and in the process, both the offenders were killed.

As a further back-up for our team, the Gujarat State Government had sought the aid of the NSG (National Security Guard) from Delhi. But the 'Black Cats' arrived only after the operation was over, and ironically, the only casualty on our side was one of the the NSGs (a Black Cat). He was injured on the next day by a huge chunk of cement which was dislodged from a concrete water tank when a colleague's automatic went off accidentally.

Life is an unpredictable game like any other, but if you do succeed in your very first operation, your self-esteem does not just soar, it grows wings! Yes, my boys had proved without doubt that they could stomach stress under fire. I was overwhelmed when they insisted that I take my share of the credit. "Khansaab was the prime motivating force," said one of them. "He leads from the front, faces gunfire with us," said another. "Can you imagine an officer of his rank dropping into a slush-filled ditch to take position? That's what Saab did. Besides, he is always available for us. We can enter his office or call him at home, anytime," gushed a third.

I guess in a world which believes that occupying a position of authority gives you the divine right to a puffed head, the hand extended by a superior in a genuine effort to trigger your dormant potential seems like an uncalled-for bonus, rather than a well-deserved gift. In this day and age, you are certainly not expected to spare a thought for your larger accountability – to society, or to your inner self. Be that as it may, for those of us who still believe that one must always give back in full measure the goodwill that one receives, the chain of mutual trust only grows stronger.

In this mutual back-patting ceremony after the Baroda operation, I had requested for the right to have the last word. When the mike was in my hand, I too spoke from the heart, telling the press, the felicitating organisations, everyone, how proud I was of the manner in which my boys had handled their first major assignment in spite of their lack of experience in the commando-warfare that this encounter had demanded.

After this confidence-boosting operation, my team successfully tackled quite a few wily gangsters (who kept getting arrested and then released because of lack of conclusive evidence) and hell-raising extortionists, who threatened people with drastic consequences if they did not pay up. How effective the ATS was may be judged from the fact that they won over twenty-three gallantry medals from the President of India in less than three years, as against the entire police force of the state, which had won only a bit more than twice the number of medals between 1947 and 1993 (which is a whole forty-six years!).

I tried to ensure though, that it was not 'all work and no play' for the boys. For instance, when we went to the police shooting range on Sundays for target practice, we carried a lot of food and made a grand picnic of it. I would also join them now and then for a drink or dinner. After all, you cannot help feeling close to people who have battled beside you, shoulder to shoulder, in life-threatening situations. Particularly when they are trying so hard to be true men of courage. Yes, my boys were always raring to go, ever willing to rise up to any challenge their demanding profession posed. They were even ready to court death, as my brave 'Jeeves' – my bodyguard Bhaskar Sonje, proved.

The terrorist network seemed to have snapped for a while after the Baroda operation, because we had eliminated three of the most wanted men of the eight-member gang, while two of them surrendered and the other three returned to Punjab. So, for almost a year and a half, all was quiet on this front. But Mumbai remained a major attraction for such extremist groups, particularly because Navi Mumbai (the newly developed industrial and residential belt connected by road and rail to the main metropolis) offered plenty of hideouts, and the many transporters who plied regularly from North India were easy fodder for the extortionist. Threatening these vulnerable folk with dire consequences to their families back home in Punjab if they did not cough up huge amounts regularly, was a lucrative option, as yet another newly-assembled gang soon discovered. They did their homework well, and knew the exact location of the kith and kin of the 'marked' transporter even before they approached him. When the lives of your loved ones are in peril, you do not squeal. You only obey, noiselessly. They knew that, all right.

Thus, after a lull, the kidnappings and murders began once again. Their callous, but flawless strategy (of warning the extortion targets that they would wipe out entire families if anyone dared to complain to the police) kept us totally in the dark about their whereabouts... till the bloody climax at a shanty town called Khendipada.

A businessman was asked to raise fifty lakh rupees within a week, if he wanted to save his family back home from total extinction. Thankfully, the terrorised man panicked and approached us for help. From his report, our team deduced where the terrorists were holed up... it was in Khendipada. An ideal location for shady operators, Khendipada was an unsightly assortment of huts spread over a hill. The illegal, cliff-top tenements had a barricade of water-pipes taller than an average man shielding them on one side, and a sheer drop on the other. What could be more convenient? Like predators ruled by jungle law, the offenders stayed invisible during the day and slunk out only after dusk to attack fresh victims.

In the seven-day reprieve they had granted this troubled informant, we began our hunt. Disguised as labourers, two bright young constables from the ATS took up residence in a hut on that hill, in order to sniff out the exact whereabouts of the dreaded gang. If they were found out, they would have paid with their lives. But like the rest of my boys, they had hearts of steel and a determination to succeed. But anxiety ran high, for the deadline was drawing near and there was not a moment to be lost. Finally, just a day before the first rendezvous, when an installment of twenty-five lakhs was to be handed over, the constables managed to locate the den – an inconspicuous dwelling on the very top of the Khendipada hill. This made fresh hope course through our veins, and steeled our resolve to get them.

May 4, 2 p.m. Two men from the ATS, playing 'driver and his colleague', drove the threatened businessman in an old Ambassador car to the meeting spot where the money was to exchange hands. We had surrounded the area with the rest of the ATS in plain clothes. The excruciating moments of waiting for the dreaded enemy began....

At about 2.30 p.m., two persons came down the hill and approached the businessman, who was standing beside the car. As per our plan, he told them that the money was with his associates in the car and asked them to bring it out. But being on the run constantly makes law-breakers develop a very sharp antenna to sense danger. As soon as the officers jumped out of the car, the two just turned and fled uphill. A wild shot rang out. Two Chinese grenades exploded. But no one was hurt and no one got caught. This was because my men had to get out of the vehicle before they could challenge the terrorists. This time-lag gave the extortionists the breather they needed to vanish uphill. Besides, the area was covered with slime, so most of the grenades flung by them landed silently in the muddy water. Coming so close to the moment of capture and then watching criminals of this stature slip through your fingers can be terribly frustrating. But as the hill offered escape only by one route, we knew they were cornered. We knew we would get them. Soon. Tonight.

By the time further reinforcements came, it was 6 p.m., and the light began to fade. We had a hurried debate over whether to surround the hillside and wait for dawn, or to go uphill immediately. Many a time, in a nerve-testing situation like this one, the momentum of an operation – the intuitive certainty that is felt unanimously about forthcoming success – becomes the decision-maker. We decided we must not, cannot give them another chance to escape. We would climb up and nab them right then.

The soil under our feet was loose, and going uphill in that unknown terrain in the growing dusk was hazardous. But our common resolve virtually put wings on our feet. Nothing could stop us now. I was wearing a bullet-proof vest over my uniform. It was snow-white in colour. When we were half-way up the hill, my bodyguard Bhaskar Sonje stopped me. "Your vest is too white, too conspicuous. Since I have the camouflage of this commando uniform, let me walk ahead of you," he said. Sonje was a tall and strapping thirty-year-old, very fit, very alert and very dedicated. I saw his point and stepped behind him. How I wish I had not....

It happened in a split second. A bullet from an AK-47 in trained hands spliced through the darkness and lodged itself in Sonje's head. His huge frame swayed, then fell. It was one of the most difficult moments of my life. I knew he was gone, but there was no time to grieve. If I had to avenge this senseless murder and bring to book the killers whose hands were already bloodied many times over, I had to take action immediately, while others took care of his body. I had lost a devoted associate. Fresh outrage surged through my entire body as I moved forward in the pitch dark that night, knowing without a shadow of doubt, that now I would get the killers up there.

We finally reached the top of the hill. By now, our eyes had got used to the darkness. Besides, we were right out in the open. So even a single light would have made sitting ducks of us too. We had already nabbed three of the five-member gang (one as he was trying to escape through the huge water-pipes and two as we were climbing up). This meant there were only two left in the tiny shelter we could roughly discern in the clearing ahead. I knew they had machine guns with ammunition belts. So there was only one way to reach them. With four of my men, I began crawling towards the back of the hut. We were armed with tear-gas shells, which we planned to shoot in through the high window on one side of the room, either by hand, or by tear-gas guns. We could hear our hearts drumming in our ears.

But we did it. Within minutes, the room was full of smoke. Then, as luck would have it, something started burning within. This made one of them rush out towards our waiting gun points. He fell in a trice, while the other succumbed to the flames within the shelter. Ironically, dying by the very fire he had played with as he chased his dubious goals. As we turned our tired feet downhill, the feeling of exultation over completing an assignment successfully was greatly dimmed by the painful awareness that a loyal teammate had contributed to this victory with his life.

The unfortunate fact about our police force today is that officers are recruited and trained mainly to work in civil zones where, in the normal course, they are only expected to maintain law and order among the citizens and be involved in crime detection. Thus, without the requisite know-how, when they are pitted against deadly 'pros' placed in volatile situations like this one, the result can be fatal, even if they have tried their best. Again, the pittance doled out as compensation to the bereaved family makes mockery of the price the man has paid by embracing death in the line of duty.

Take the case of Sonje, who died on the hill that night. He had a five-year-old son and a twenty-five-year-old wife expecting their second baby. Left to fend for themselves, this family would have been in dire straits all too soon. To prevent this unfair denouement, I decided to start a trust fund for them. Apart from my men, the transporters, who were very grateful to have these deadly extortionists removed from their path, came forward readily to contribute towards the welfare of Sonje's family. We opened a bank account in the wife's name and within a month, collected about eight lakh rupees. To erase all suspicions that we may be misappropriating the money, we insisted that all donations should be made by cheque in the name of the young widow. We also approached the government for help, and managed to get her a flat in a colony developed by its housing board.

We make a living by what we get,
but we make a life by what we give.
Winston Churchill

Like all mothers, Mrs. Sonje was very keen to educate her son in a good school. We had heard of a very good public school at Deolali (a military base a few hours' run from Mumbai). One of our assistant commissioners and an officer were sent there to talk to the principal. The kind-hearted man not only admitted the boy, he also waived the fee along with the charges for boarding and lodging.

The generosity of the grateful transporters and my colleagues in the force, as also the laudable gesture of the principal of the

Deolali Public School, proved yet again, that most law-abiding human beings just need the right curtain-puller to reveal the large-hearted philanthropist tucked away within. When an entire community comes forward in this manner to alleviate the pain of an individual, organised society becomes so much more than just a heated race of multiple talents competing selfishly for first place. It becomes a nurturing nest where one can heal in peace, until one is ready to face the fresh battles ahead.

CHAPTER FIVE

A CLASSROOM CALLED 'LIFE'

Do you have a few close friends? Or at least one, who knows you inside out? A friend who will happily float with you on the clouds of lazy, crazy dreams and also hold your hand at those sub-human moments, when the mercury of your mood dips to freezing point? A friend with whom you can share a risqué joke, or the comforting blanket of silence with equal ease? I mean, someone who knows your true worth, your kinks and 'chinks', and can offer a timely tip without trespassing or sounding meddlesome? Do you have a friend as invaluable, as real as that? If you do, then you know why I want to relive these moments, why I wish to unwrap these memories....

True friendship is like sound health, the value of 'it' is seldom known until it be lost.

Charles Caleb Colton

I met my first close friend when I was in the third grade. His name was Rocky, and together we weathered many an adolescent storm until we passed out of school. Whether it was on our bicycles, in the classroom cooking up wild pranks, or on the playground, Rocky and I were inseparable. We were teammates even in the cricket matches that we played for our alma mater. But after letting us bask in the carefree sunshine of those glorious, growing years, destiny planned different destinations for the two of us. I graduated from college and joined the Police Academy, while he opted to become a priest. Come to think of it, there is still a common thread binding the goals that Rocky and I finally chose. Both of us, in a sense, set out to launder the wide world outside – me in my no-nonsense uniform, with my baton and gun, trying to clean the streets 'without' of criminals of all species, and he in his soothing robes, with his gentle sermons, trying to cleanse individual hearts of the demons lurking 'within'. Yet another proof of the ultimate unity in diversity.

My next band of close-knit chums was formed at the Police Academy. As I have mentioned before, our days there were hard and long, beginning at an unearthly 4.45 a.m.! This was the first time that many of us, who had led a fairly charmed existence through school and college, learnt to cope with a rigid schedule that literally kept us on our toes. The biggest thorn in our victimised sides was a huge and fierce Irishman, who seemed to actually enjoy doling out tough 'sentences' even if we committed the 'offence' of falling ill! Now this was a bit too much, and naturally, our young blood boiled over. So one day, three of us put our indignant heads together and hatched a typical greenhorn's plan to teach the towering inferno a lesson.

On the following morning, when the tyrant was curtly supervising our 5.15 a.m. jog, we 'accidentally' bumped into him and succeeded in toppling him over. True, our childish revenge might seem totally incongruous with the ideals of the noble profession we were being sculpted for. I can almost hear you say, "How could future protectors behave like such juvenile violators?" But, being otherwise powerless to tackle this unjust individual, our entire batch felt that our successful mission of getting our own back by sending our common enemy sprawling on his, was completely justified. I must add that the cheap thrill of that morning's 'comic drill' gave all of us a high that enabled us to sail through our tough timetable for days after!

Yes, it is perfectly natural, even for a normally balanced and obedient individual, to break out into erratic behaviour when provoked by a superior who misuses both position and power without realising the drastic and far-reaching effect this can have on those under his, or her command. This indelible fact was brought home to me years later, when history repeated itself in my own home....

"Could you please come over some time today? We... I mean my vice-principal has had a... er... a problem with your younger son," said the principal of the school, where both my boys – Mansoor and Zaheer – were studying. Promising to drop in as soon as I could, I put the receiver down, wondering what could have gone wrong.

Yes, my sons are by nature high-spirited, but I have always considered that to be a blessing. For it has enabled them to take the highs and lows of my being in the public glare in their stride. For instance, during my anti-terrorist drives, when I made quite a few enemies among the 'most wanted' clan, my children had to get used to abnormal rules like not going out or returning at the same time each day (meaning, not creating a pattern or timetable that any secret observer may misuse). They have been shunted between personal and official cars often, made to travel with me in unmarked vehicles to avoid detection, and so on. Once, when Mansoor had not even stepped into his teens, he picked up the phone only to hear a dreaded terrorist (whom I shot later) growl, "Your dad has been quite a pest, young man. He has killed a lot of my men. Tell him to lay off, or I will finish him off myself... with my own bare hands!" Now this is not a sentence a child can instantly give retort to. But believe it or not, Mansoor actually shouted back at the cruel fanatic. "If you think you are so strong, then come and get him," he invited, mustering up a bravado he must have scarcely felt. Even as my throat tightened, my heart had ballooned with pride on that day. I felt I was the luckiest father in the whole world. I felt like my little son was my buddy who understood what I was all about, in spite of the harsh fact that I was guilty of not always 'being there' when my family needed me.

This happens often, because a policeman works more on the days when his fellow citizens are on holiday, celebrating India's many festivals, or out on the streets protesting about something... anything. But how can one explain the meaning of grown-up words like "the call of duty" to a little child who is missing his dad? Yet, I must admit that my children never, ever complained about my being a father in absentia. Nor did they take undue advantage of the perks my uniform fetched them. For example, if I ever offered to drop them off at school on my way to work, they would never let me reach them right up to the gates in my official vehicle. I had to drop them at an invisible street corner and let them walk the rest of the way. *So what could Zaheer have done today to invite the wrath of his vice-principal and summon my presence immediately?* I asked myself this question yet again as I got out of my car and walked into the school building.

"Your son entered my vice-principal's office in her absence, and flung her keys and other belongings out of the third-floor window," said the principal in a measured tone that scarcely disguised the anger he felt.

I could not believe my ears. Both my boys enjoyed school immensely and also took part in many an inter-school sports tournament. Being an outdoors person myself, I have always been particular about regular exercise, and not a day begins without a few sets of badminton. A day on which there is no time for a work-out, is a day lost on my fitness calendar. Naturally, I have tried to inculcate the same traits in my children too. Whenever I was in town during their growing years, I would always pull them out for an early morning jog before they got ready for school. That was our quality time for communicating 'man-to-man'. So in spite of not being a twenty-four-hour parent (and barring a few spicy tales that children share only with their loyal, tight-lipped moms), I was pretty confident that there were no walls between me and my fairly normal sons... and now? My son, who was quite a water baby, who shone on the badminton court at both the junior and senior-level meets, had done this? No, no, couldn't be. There must be a mistake somewhere. Why, even today he had left early because he was going with his sports teacher to represent the school in javelin throw. So then, what prompted him to return to school and play such a spiteful prank? I demanded to know more.

The vice-principal was sent for, as also my defensive son. Slowly, the pieces of the puzzle began to fall into place. Zaheer had actually returned jubilant from the inter-school competition, where he had won third prize. However, because he reached school a little later than normal, he had had no time to change his footwear before the morning assembly. The victory and consequent honour he had brought for his school had obviously meant nothing to the vice-principal, who rebuked him for being in his sports shoes, and ordered him to keep them in her office and move around barefoot all day as a punishment.

I do not have to paraphrase the storm that this cold and unjust command must have raised in an angry, but helpless little boy's heart. So what did he do? He walked up three floors barefoot and put salve on his wound with an act of childish revenge.

I tried asking the vice-principal why she had not sent Zaheer home, if she felt he should be reprimanded for being improperly dressed. I tried pointing out to her that the boy may have retaliated in this bizarre fashion because he felt terribly hurt that instead of being congratulated for his success, he had actually been humiliated in front of the entire school. Madam's demand that a child should not be in sports shoes for the morning assembly was right, but the timing, in Zaheer's case, had been absolutely wrong. I even tried telling her that whenever I catch one of my subordinates napping, I call him to my room and reprimand him in private, rather than pulling him up in front of his colleagues. This way, the man has a chance to tell his side of the story and also to reflect upon where he has gone wrong.

But the vice-principal was too self-absorbed, too furious to even listen to (forget understanding) what I had to say. All she could see before her smarting gaze was an audacious child, who had flung her belongings (the vice-principal's personal property, no less), out of the window! Not to mention an equally audacious father, who seemed unperturbed by such an act of devilry. As I stared at the frozen, venomous look on that annoyed woman's face, she transformed before my very eyes into that dictatorial Irishman who had enjoyed being merciless with my batch all those years ago at the Police Academy. I really had to try hard at that moment to play the reproached parent. Given half a chance, I would have loved to gleefully recount the equally 'sad' retaliation received by my Police Academy trainer, and then guffaw, "Like father, like son, ha-ha," before walking out of that stuffy office on that day!

Jokes apart, I seriously feel that if man management is a fine art, child management is a finer art. It is only when you have unlimited patience, poise, loads of self-discipline (in terms of practicing what you preach), a sympathetic ear, and an 'open heart', that you can aspire to command respect, rather than having to demand it. A fact that, unfortunately, does not penetrate the dense fog covering any mind that is intoxicated by the power that comes as a heady bonus when you become a parent, or reach the upper rungs of any ladder.

Friends come in every size, every disguise; age, class, caste, no bar. The trick is to keep an open mind to receive them, enjoy them, and benefit from the wisdom they have acquired before reaching the threshold of your home and heart. This thought reminds me of a memorable lesson I learnt many summers ago, from someone who was a senior colleague.

During the probation period following the rigorous training at the Police Academy, it is customary to put a trainee in charge of a police station as an S.H.O. (Station House Officer), in order to test his ability to function independently. Thus, I was asked to go to Vaijapur, a fairly big police station in the interior of the State of Maharashtra. My senior superintendent must have sensed that I was too raw to handle such a large police station on my own, so he suggested that I take an experienced officer with me. I jumped at the idea and requested for a witty veteran named Kulkarni. I quite liked this seasoned old man, who had often regaled me with colourful tales of how he had arrested some desperate gangs of dacoits in his heyday. My superintendent had a slight smile on his face as he nodded his approval of my choice.

I must confess that I felt a wee bit puffed up about being handed the reins of an entire station. Any fresher would feel the same, if he alighted from the train at the Vaijapur station to find a staff van and quite a few policemen waiting to welcome and then take him, in a ceremonious procession, to the headquarters. The existing S.H.O. was normally asked to take his annual vacation during these 'trial runs', this 'breaking-in' process of a new recruit, but that did not faze me. I was quite confident I could handle the assignment smoothly... but that was about to change.

There I was, sitting on my 'throne' of justice, flanked on one side by the S.H.O. who was about to proceed on leave, and on the other by my wise *guru*, Kulkarni, when an agitated villager rushed in gasping, *"Gazab ho gaya, main lut gaya!"* (A terrible thing has happened, I have been robbed!). I realised, with a quickening pulse, that it was me he was addressing. For the first time, I was in charge of dispensing justice to an obviously wronged individual. I heard myself asking him to sit down.

From the incoherent babble that poured forth from his indignant voice, I pieced together his sad story: the man was a hireling, who had been given three hundred rupees by his master (the landlord), either to deposit in the bank, or to fetch some supplies. On his way, the poor chap had met his fate in the form of two slick conmen. In front of his spellbound eyes, he saw one of them hand over a ten-rupee note to the other, who held it in his closed fist and 'prayed' over it. He then (apparently) stuffed the note into a cigarette pack and handed it over to the first man with loud instructions that he should open it only after he had walked a distance of hundred metres, without looking back! When the 'receiver' came bounding back waving the doubled booty – 'two' ten-rupee notes that had emerged from the pack – our ignoramus had been won over! Fully convinced that this magician had the power to double his money too, he foolishly handed over the entire three hundred rupees. Predictably, when he obediently walked the hundred metres without a backward glance and then opened the pack, it was woefully empty.

By then the partners in crime were nowhere in sight. "Please help me find those rogues, or I am done for!" the cheated farmhand wailed, with folded hands.

Feeling sorry for the poor labourer and displaying typical freshman-frenzy, I immediately sent out some of my men to scour the bus stands and the railway station, but to no avail. The tricksters had vanished without a trace. As I fumbled with my vocabulary, trying to console the distraught chap, my mentor, Kulkarni said: "Most people do not get any wiser even after plodding through a lifetime. Be grateful that you learnt a lesson for life at the cost of a mere three hundred rupees!" I am sure that poor fellow never fell into the trap laid by a glib trickster ever again. And to tell you the truth, neither did I.

I will not be telling you the whole story if I do not talk about my closest friends – the hills. Yes, I love their majestic stature, much above the strife and grime of a mechanised, man-made world. I love their un-peopled heights. I love the splendid isolation they offer me. I also love the fact that they keep their cool even at the peak of summer. Nestling in their silent companionship, the wounds inflicted by the gruesome facts I grapple with in my day-to-day life heal faster, introspection comes easier. Some of the loveliest memories I have are of the mountains to the west of Sikkim. I stayed there, with just a brilliant cook for company, in a forest rest-house from where one had to travel at least five kilometres for basic provisions.

Managing, with some difficulty, to get hold of a guide, I remember stepping out one morning at 4 a.m., for an unforgettable three-hour climb. The higher I went, the finer the air I breathed and the farther I left behind those 'irrelevant' heavy burdens that make mincemeat of body, mind and spirit. At break of dawn, we were at the very source of the volatile River Teesta. There was no checked tablecloth to unfold, no dainty picnic basket to uncover. Just unlimited servings of the purest air to breathe, natural mineral water to quench one's thirst with, and yes, a heart full of gratitude for this privileged, private rendezvous.

I have also had some memorable vacations in solitary cottages along the lochs of Scotland. This is the kind of place to which one carries cartons of unread books, a rare malt whisky, a favourite pipe, a 'do not disturb' placard, and hopes to find an armchair to bury oneself in. In those lush, virgin acres, the spoken word is a scarce commodity, thank God! You can actually walk a few kilometres here without meeting a soul, and even if you do, you can just move on with a slight nod or smile. Peace of mind, the one luxury you cannot bid for or buy over a counter, befriends you instantly in such a sanctuary. Keeping both work pressures and the multi-spangled chaos of digital entertainment at bay, one can listen to one's true inner voice, or just revel in the rejuvenating embrace of silence.

Not that I always think like a hermit when planning a holiday, oh no! I love to sniff out undiscovered getaways, or make idle chat with strangers who turn into family over a couple of tankards of ale in noisy and nondescript pubs – the only hot-spots of many an unknown small town. I fondly remember Swords (no, in spite of my 'steely' profession, that name has nothing to do with my choice of weapon!). Swords is a picturesque village, a few hours out of Dublin. I have really enjoyed its untrammelled beauty – the gentle hiss of the breeze swishing through swaying willows, the endless emerald meadows, and a swift-moving river on whose bank I lay breathless, but in total, unhindered bliss.

Another dream-destination I can never forget is Spiddles (now that is quite an unforgettable name, isn't it?). Spiddles is an absolutely delightful village in Ireland. It was recommended to me by the attendant at a gas station, and I am so glad I took his tip. Tiny shops line its roads and almost every second one is (you guessed it!) a pub. The bed 'n breakfast we chose, was run by a middle-aged couple. It had cosy rooms on top, with a roomy lounge on the ground floor. Bernie Thornton, the lady of the house, remains high on my list of unforgettable people, both for her incredible Irish tea and her exhaustive knowledge of Irish history. I have always thought I am considerably well-informed on this subject, but two hours with

Bernie made me realise how many gaps there were in my data-book. If you are a true student, there is no end to learning, is there?

Besides Irish history, Bernie and her husband taught my wife, my daughter, and me a rather strenuous native game played on the village green, using what looked, roughly, like hockey sticks. We also went pub-crawling with the Thorntons. One evening, we were at one of these joints where everyone knows everyone else, when this lovely and happily-sozzled girl walked in. Two blokes, probably handymen who were unwinding after a hard day, let pass a sleazy remark and we were quite taken aback to hear that pretty mouth shut them up with an earful of unmentionables, which actually made the red-cheeked twosome shuffle out of the door. Now that was something. I stepped across to speak to her.

Even in that semi-stupor, she must have sensed that I did not spell more trouble, for she told me her name was Michaela and that she worked for a local TV station. She also candidly confessed that she was penniless when we asked her to join us for a Chinese dinner. Interestingly, before she left the pub with us, Michaela downed a few glasses of iced water (to get her feet back on *terra firma*), and then proved to be great company for the rest of that enjoyable evening.

Looking for a moral in my Spiddles story? Just think about it... right from the chirpy attendant at the gas station, to the multi-faceted Mama Thornton, and finally, the dead-sober but extremely lively Michaela, there is an endless ocean of invaluable teachers out there. They may be tucked away in unknown places. They may wear inconspicuous faces. They may do insignificant jobs. But each carries a special surprise for you. The trick is to try and develop a heart that is able to see and listen as well!

Speaking of listening takes me back to the remote areas of India, which I had to tour extensively, whenever I was the superintendent in charge of an entire district. My portfolio demanded that I visit every police station under my command at least once a year, and spend four days listening to the locals' grievances. On these visits one normally stayed at guesthouses providing basic amenities, some creaky furniture, and thankfully, an ancient '*khansama*' (you cannot call him a mere cook, he is more like a walking encyclopedia). It is from this vanishing breed of buddies that I have heard some of the most colourful titbits about the little world they inhabit.

Many a night has stretched itself out on those wide porticos of forest rest-houses, as I watched the light and shade of the hurricane lamp weave a delicate tapestry on the animated face of the *khansama* and listened to crickets chirp like punctuation marks, as he hopped, merrily, from one story to another. Often, my mind had to swing like a dizzy pendulum while my raconteur's time machine carried me decades back in time, to dwell upon memories of the colonial era, and then brought me back with a jolt, to the quirks of a present-day, local goon. Sometimes, I would mention a problem I was facing and the wizened man squatting before me would offer an intriguing point of view springing from a grassroots perspective. Yes, I do enjoy the comforts life has presented me with. But no red-carpeted seven-star hotel has ever offered me that incomparable companionship, that 'at-home' feeling that comes from sharing time and space with someone who belongs to a totally different world, but lights a little lamp in your own with his quaint charm, his eagerness to please, his story-telling skills, or his ability to share sound or silence at rickety rest-houses in 'faraway places with strange-sounding names'.

To switch from remote destinations to an internationally known state in India, take Kashmir. Wearing the Himalayas like a dazzling crown, Kashmir was a beauteous queen in the pageant of India's multi-cultural states, till the clouds of fear and hatred spawned by mindless terrorism crowded out all its rainbow colours and natural glory. How different, how enticing the 'climate' of this chosen land was, once upon a time. How can I forget the peace we had basked in, many summers ago, when we went fishing in the swift-flowing river at Sonmarg? Or recreate the glow that bathed our every cell as we reclined with faces upturned to a blue sheet of sky, after a superb breakfast of the fresh trout we had just caught?

Nature is, without doubt, the most denigrated and yet the most devoted friend you can ever have on earth. In an instant, she wipes away the ill-effects of the cosmetic overdrive which exhausts, and finally kills you as you try desperately to live up to your overblown self-image. She helps you to hear your real self speak... and then, she listens without interruption. All artifice melts, all pretensions dissolve in her pristine presence. You begin to see, to accept, and then combat your limitations. You realise that your real enemy is not the one raging outside of you, but the one who beguiles, seduces, and overpowers you from within.

Nature's tenacity, her fortitude, teaches by example how to cultivate a still centre... so that you unlearn the desire to 'become' something; so that you discover the lasting joy that comes from simply 'being'.

There is a pleasure in the pathless woods,
There is a rapture on the lonely shore,
There is a society where none intrudes,
By the deep sea and music in its roar:
I love not man the less, but nature more.

Lord Byron

CHAPTER SIX

ALL IN A DAY'S WORK

"This is Inspector Patil from the Colaba Police Station. Your son had an accident near the Maker Arcade. He was rushed to Jaslok Hospital and given twelve stitches to his head." The line went dead. Even as I jumped out of bed, switched on the light, and began changing into whatever I could lay my hands on, a furious battery of thoughts tried to make sense of what I had just heard. While my mind began to remind me: *Yes, my younger son had gone out on his motor-bike earlier in the evening... he has not returned yet... and it is 1.30 a.m. now!*

F.E.A.R. = False Evidence Appearing Real.

Anthony Robbins

Did that mean... was it true... oh my God! The flustered dad in me wanted to fly out barefoot in the dark to be near my son. While the composed professional, schooled for years not to crumble under pressure, began piecing together the information. Colaba Police Station? Maker Arcade? Jaslok? The three places were in different areas. No, no, NO, something was not quite jelling here. Suddenly the light-shaft of reason pierced through the dark clouds of paternal fear. I stopped buttoning my shirt to lift the phone and dial the control room at the police headquarters. Had they received any intimation of an accident at Maker Arcade? Didn't that complex fall under the jurisdiction of the Cuffe Parade Police Cell? Then how did the

Colaba Station get wind of the incident first? Most important, was there an Inspector Patil at Colaba?

This rapid round of questions, fired from a mind that was back in the calm lane, yielded the expected answers. No, there had been no accident reported, Maker Arcade did not come under the Colaba Cell, and last but not the least, there was no Inspector Patil at Colaba. Obviously therefore, the whole thing had been an ugly ruse on the part of some shady operators to get me out of the house, alone and defenceless in the dead of the night. Fabricated to settle some score in an unscrupulous manner, no doubt. But since 'sense and sensibility' had averted that danger, there was no point in dwelling upon what may have happened had I stepped out. While there was a major point in favour of my going back to bed! Which I did. Especially, since my son actually walked in at that very moment, saying what a great party he had been to (and nowhere near the Maker Arcade, either)!

Being in the hot seat means being continually on a red alert to sniff out unsettling misinformation like this. Or worse still, to tackle ugly encounters when you actually meet different brands of fugitives face to face. A meeting which may have drastic consequences for the offender, or the captor. And yet ironically, there is a terrible stigma attached to the word 'encounter'. Even if it results in the death of notorious criminals, the general feeling is that the police had an ulterior motive in 'finishing them off'.

Now, what exactly is an encounter? An encounter means a situation wherein the police comes upon a wanted man either by accident, or based upon information received. The criminals nabbed on such occasions are ones who have either committed a heinous offence, or have assembled to do so. If they are armed, the police has to perforce, retaliate. If a desperado's gun is pointing straight at you, you cannot wait until he fires, can you? Yet the general suspicion is that the man was probably picked up elsewhere, and then summarily eliminated.

I have always countered such questionable sympathy for notorious public enemies very firmly. My argument is that since the underworld has never threatened or targeted members of the Indian police force directly, why should people assume that we bear any special animosity towards them, or harbour a cheap desire for vendetta by questionable means? One must not forget that the man in uniform actually puts his life on the line each time he takes on a hardened criminal. Taking a risk from which he stands to gain nothing – nothing personal, nothing material. So where is the question of attributing underhand motives to his action? A policeman is a normal human being, not a psychopath who enjoys killing without a conscience. Yes, I agree that at times, some officers overreact, caught up in the excitement of the moment. But to say that all encounters are fake is a damaging allegation that can make the policeman's morale plummet. Not fair, considering the fact that he is forever engaged in cleaning up all that is foul in society.

Of course, people do applaud our efforts when there is a major crackdown and a lot of bad guys who have been a menace to society are apprehended. But the same public raised a hue and cry when two sharpshooter aides of a well-known don were accosted and killed when they were trying to get away in a cab. Did the protestors know how many cases were pending against these criminals? Were they aware of the hapless condition of the bereaved mothers, wives, or sisters of the innocents that these toughies had mercilessly done away with? Equally important, did they have any idea of how many policemen had died in such dangerous encounters? Had these 'lopsided' sympathisers ever thought of crusading on behalf of *their* families? Why not?

Handling these trying dilemmas in addition to normal policing work kept my plate full during my days as additional commissioner. After a couple of brisk sets on the badminton court, I would reach my office by nine o'clock every morning. The day began with collating and coordinating special operations, and supervising the functioning of the twenty-nine police stations under my wing. Meanwhile, a steady stream of information kept pouring in about different kinds of crimes being committed all over the metropolis, and of stray disruptions of law and order. Surprise visits had to be made to a few police cells every day to check the condition of the lock-up (to ensure no one had been jailed on false grounds or unduly harassed).

Back at my desk, it was time to meet about twenty or thirty policemen with personal problems like an un-repaid loan, a domestic emergency, or anything that needed the helpful intervention of the 'head of their family' who had both a willing ear, and the authority to render the desired assistance. After these friendly *tête-à-têtes,* a myriad of administrative problems swallowed up the hours till the lunch break. The entire afternoon was devoted to meeting laypersons who had applied beforehand for time to spell out their grievances. By and large, these were civil disputes like encroachment on property, a theft, or some domestic squabble. This was followed by a brainstorming session with my officers over some special issues, including forecasting the likely 'weather on the street' on the following day, especially if there was a likelihood of any labour or communal strife, or any form of religious congregation or procession. In such cases, an officer from that area would request for extra manpower.

Finally, it was the turn of the senior inspectors who needed advice for processing cases booked under *TADA.* While the legal officer on the staff prepared a précis of each, the decision about how to deal with it had to be taken by me. Perhaps it was a deep awareness of the authority of the chair I occupied, along with a strong commitment to the responsibility that it carried, that helped me sail through all of this without getting too ruffled. I also believe that physical fitness contributes greatly to mental alertness. Without those few games of badminton at the club, I would have felt worn out at the end of a working day. That would have made it difficult to accept or enjoy the social obligations – the requests to address social organisations, the many dinner invitations – which are a 'must' when you are in public service and which are invariably held on weekdays! Now that requires extending yourself a bit when your average working day winds up only after 9 p.m.!

What I am trying to drive home is the fact that the police force cannot function in a vacuum. A lot of valuable information comes to us from the general public, and unless we are constantly in touch with them, how will they know what we are capable of and why will they feel motivated to come forward and cooperate with us? Meeting the world outside helps to create our indispensable chain of informers. But the media attention we inevitably get tends to arouse a lot of envy, and we often end up being vilified. Brutality, corruption, and high-handedness are some of the charges we have to face constantly. But that is because we are in a profession in which whatever we do affects the common man directly. For instance, if you are in a tearing hurry and jump the lights at a traffic signal to zoom ahead, you get miffed with the traffic cop who accosts you for that trespass, don't you? And when you try to avoid any laborious process of the law by greasing a palm or two, do you ever feel guilty?

I am not saying that cops never slip up. Whenever an inquiry officer presented recorded evidence of absence from duty, or drunkenness, or any form of on-the-job corruption, conducting a departmental investigation and implementing the required punishment (a fine, reduction in pay or rank, or even compulsory retirement if need be) was part of my administrative portfolio. Even if there was some form of arm-twisting attempted by an influential lobby, I always stuck to my guns and did what had to be done on the basis of the evidence. When you occupy a top position, credibility does not come overnight. You have to strive to first create it, and then retain it at all times.

That was about inside stories. But interacting with the outside world helps the force to place its own problems before society and make it aware of the shackles that come in the way of our smooth functioning. This way, the common man realises how much his cooperation can help. Just as every little piece fits in to complete a jigsaw, it is only when everyone does his bit that a social framework can become strong and capable of withstanding divisive forces trying to cause a rent from the outside.

> *There is really no such creature as a single individual; he has no more life of his own than a cast-off cell marooned from the surface of your skin.*
>
> Lewis Thomas

After the Baroda operation, which made a lot of headlines and created an upsurge of faith in our ability, many people started telephoning us anonymously with tip-offs. Even if ninety percent of these were false trails, the ten percent that were genuine provided vital clues to spur on several investigations. In fact, I would say that most of the success we had in rounding up terrorists or gangsters was because of the unseen help rendered by our informers.

To add to this 'bank', and to give different sections of society the chance to interface with the 'cutting edge' of the force (the sub-inspectors and inspectors with whom they come in touch whenever there is a problem), we began organising regular meetings twice a week. This gave ordinary people like clerks, secretaries, factory workers, government and hospital staff, a chance to find out what makes a policeman rude on occasion and what causes bad vibes between the man on the street and the man in uniform. At each of these open houses, about twenty police officers cleared the doubts of about two hundred invitees from different organisations.

While helping greatly to boost the faith of the common man in our good intentions, this practice was also an eye-opener for us in many ways. For instance, a woman advocate, who had been ignored by one errant officer when she had rushed to complain about a snatched purse, ended up nursing a bias against the entire force till this meeting cleared the air and changed her perspective! Again, there are many instances of murders in broad daylight in public places, when the shopkeepers, who were direct witnesses, downed shutters and insisted they had not seen a thing. "Now where can the police go with a grievance like that?" we asked our audience.

Sometimes, ignorance of the workings of a police cell can lead to a wrong impression about us. For instance, every police station has two duty officers in the night. Each of them has to register any complaint that comes in, and visit the problem site. When too many offences are committed in a single night, obviously someone is kept waiting. A person who was terribly annoyed that he was kept waiting for over an hour when he rushed to the police station at 12.30 a.m. after his chain was snatched, realised at one of our gatherings that it was overburdening and not cussedness that had prevented the officer on duty from attending to him immediately. Many such misgivings were cleared because of these regular meetings.

Junior officers in the police force also experience a lot of stress as they are forever being badgered with deadlines by their superior, to tie up the forty or fifty cases pending in each station at any given time. In addition to this, these cogs in the wheel have to also do patrolling, night duty, put in extra hours during festivals or visits of dignitaries without any extra pat on the back, because promotions come very slowly. When the working day keeps getting longer, the average policeman has no time for family, and sometimes resorts to the bottle, which causes further heartache to his near ones.

If hard work pays, stress gets balanced. The heightened sense of accomplishment experienced by a senior officer as a result of the public appreciation his efforts earn him, offsets all the negative offshoots of the load he carries. Looking back, I can tell you that there can be no greater reward. At a function organised at a suburb where we had managed to overpower some deadly criminals, I was overwhelmed by a fan who had actually compiled an entire file of press cuttings recording our success stories. She was the mother of a successful film star, but this was the first time I had met her. Tell me, when life whips up such unexpected morale-boosting snifters, can one's adrenaline ask for more?

But those are just bonus points that add a surprise spark to this unique journey. What contributes the substance is having a meticulously drawn work-plan and a strong set of principles that will set it in smooth motion. Principles that take into account both your duties as a worker, and your responsibilities as a team-leader, if you happen to be one. This reminds me of a recent incident when a chap at the club thought I was loony because I was fretting about being late for work. "Hey, you can't be serious. You are heading your own set-up now. Whom do you have to report to, huh?" he grinned.

He was not all wrong. My days in the police force are over, and today I am answerable only to myself in the organisation I head. But he was not all right either. For, if I do not follow the rules I have drawn up, if I do not maintain a strict code of discipline myself, how can I enforce it on others?

CHAPTER SEVEN

ON THE ROAD TO PERDITION

There are two kinds of dreamers. You may prefer to call them escapists, because of their innate inability to digest reality-bytes unless they are garnished liberally with rainbow dressing.

Take a devoted housewife for example, who goes through her uninterrupted grind, day in and day out, for years, decades. You never catch her slipping. You never hear her wishing she could hand over the keys of this monotonous kingdom to someone else. But then, you also never know that she drowns her ennui in a daily 'fix' of tear-jerking television soaps or 'happy-ever-after' romances. Or take any man from the hordes of humanity crowding streets, bus stops, railway platforms. He chases his daily bread with dogged determination, in an ill-ventilated cubby-hole at an inconspicuous office. You cannot remember how he looks, even if you travel by the same public transport. You do not know what he likes to eat, or where he shops for special occasions. You are also not aware that our man never, ever misses a Jackie Chan, Schwarzenegger, Van Damme (or now, Vin Diesel!) movie. Or, that he gets his 'happy hour' kick from watching WWF or FTV after the rest of the family has gone to bed. These two random examples comprise the majority of voyeurs, whose harmless flights of fancy actually help them to live amicably, to make peace with the padlocks that keep their feet fastened firmly upon mother earth.

Much more greedy, callous, and therefore deadly, is the dreamer of the other kind. He is the one who wants to get rich in a hurry.

He believes the end justifies the means. So, he plays dangerous games for high stakes. He takes his 'hunting' orders, most of the time, from a boss he never meets. He may visualise a retired life of peace and plenty awaiting him at the other end of the mean street he operates from. But before he reaches that utopia, he generally gets caught in the web he has woven himself... ruining many lives besides his own on the way to carrying out the plans of his misguided master. He is the dreaded contract killer, who calls a willful murder a 'job' and charges blood money for every life he takes!

The latter half of the year 1989 saw a sudden outburst of gang-wars between the puppet armies of mafia overlords who, more often than not, remote-controlled their 'elimination manoeuvres' from cozy, foreign locations. Since the common man was initially unaffected by this private rivalry and bloodshed, I did not mind it. In fact, I was rather happy, because I felt that this was nature's way of repaying action with reaction. I felt this was the master-plan of someone up there, to clean the city of some of these troublemaking hoodlums.

But soon their capers began to threaten normal life in the city. The daredevils began to openly show more muscle, they began to get more brazen. When a policeman guarding one such arrested gangster at a local municipal hospital located in a crowded area was killed by the members of a rival party in an abortive attempt to finish off the 'sick' don, we decided we had had enough. It was time to de-weed, time to systematically track down these bloodhounds, and calm the panic they had begun to generate among ordinary people.

These were the kinds of crimes the ATS was created to tackle. The advantage the ATS members had, was that they had the time to build up a huge network of contacts, and then utilise this vast and widespread machinery to collect source material, to gather information about the whereabouts of all the top-guns on the police force's 'most wanted' list. This kind of classified information normally comes from three sources. The first of these is the paid informer. He may be a pickpocket, a small-time criminal like a cat-burglar, or even a bootlegger whose survival instinct prompts him to keep his eyes and ears open. By passing on a tip about what they have seen or heard, these *chhota pegs* of petty mischief try to stay within the good books of the local police. This is how the force comes to know if there is anyone being terrorised or victimised in a particular area, or if there is a new 'brat' on the block who needs to be monitored closely.

The second kind of informer is one who volunteers information out of spite, or an injured ego, to wreak revenge on his enemy. This kind of data needs to be properly scrutinised, because it may be spiced up by a shrewd mind with an axe to grind, by a crook seeking the support of a public agency to engineer a private vendetta.

The third and rarer species of police-aide is the honourable, socially aware and alert citizen, who approaches you with some titbit he has picked up, in a spirit of public service. Normally, laypersons prefer to keep their noses out of trouble. Even if they have witnessed a crime, they feign ignorance, out of indifference or a fear of reprisal from the unknown and unscrupulous enemy at large, or because of the conviction that the police are always hand-in-glove with the criminals. This major misconception about the credibility of the police force was laid to rest on a dramatic November afternoon at Lokhandwala (a densely populated residential complex in a western suburb of Mumbai).

At 1 p.m., the phone in my specially-created ATS office rang. The call was from a mole of the second order, a petty gangster-turned-informer who generally knew what he was talking about, because prior to his dropping out, he too used to report to a well-known don. He was such a suspicious and nervy character, that he would not even speak to any of my officers. I have often met this twilight person alone, in the lonely car park of a five-star hotel in the dead of the night; or in the packed out-patient department of a municipal hospital, only to keep his fears at bay and get even one measly nugget of underworld news that would help me to bring yet another offender to book. The common man never realises how often policemen have to do such unconventional and danger-ridden things, just to trap one slippery criminal. Today he had called me on my direct line, and yet the wariness, born of years of dodging arrest, made him wait for my "Hello," before he spoke.

"I have spotted at least seven of the rats you are looking for. They are holed up in a ground-floor flat at Lokhandwala. They lugged in what seemed like a huge cache of weapons, from two cars. They have parked their vehicles right in front of the two entrances to the building. Just in case they have to beat it, you understand? So come and get them, hurry!" The guy was speaking in short rasps, as if he feared the very walls of the phone booth would mow him down for opening his mouth.

"But who are they and who is their target? What more do you know about the operation? And yes, give me their exact location," I persisted.

"All I can tell you is that they are after some builders, who have not coughed up the promised money. All kinds of swanky cars keep coming and going from this place. I hear there is even a kidnapping of a builder's son in the offing. Just note down this address... and rush down... after all, it isn't everyday that you get a tip-off about the whereabouts of Maya Dolas, eh?" The line died in my hand and my fingers froze on the receiver.

Maya Dolas... fearsome hit-man, extortionist, and core-member of the widespread gang of a well-known Dubai-based don. For a man who sported a name that is (in Hindu spiritual parlance) synonymous with all that binds, attaches, holds you captive to the ties of this grand illusion called life, 'Maya' was one free bird. For not only had he snapped bonds with all that is good and virtuous, not only could he endlessly harass and torture people for money, not only did he mercilessly snuff out men from rival gangs, he had also escaped from the clutches of justice by assaulting the police guarding him on his way back to prison from a court hearing. This escape was, of course, accomplished with help from his equally cold-blooded cronies. Today, that much-wanted Maya Dolas along with his prized henchmen was just a few kilometres, just a half-hour's ride away from the boomerang of justice. It seemed like pay-up time.

Immediately, I summoned all the nine ATS men present in the office at the time. A moment wasted was a moment lost. “Go just now and surround the place. I will follow on your heels with the rest of the team. We must not, cannot, will not let Dolas get away this time. Come on, let’s move,” I told my boys, even as I started dialing frantically for additional forces.

The palpable sense of foreboding at the scene of action was like a straight lift from a Hollywood thriller. My boys had surveyed the area on padded feet before I got there. We were stealthily closing in on the side entrance of the apartment house when an unexpected outburst of fire caught us absolutely by surprise. One of my men got a bullet in the chest, another in his knee. Even as I ensured that they were both whisked away in a police vehicle to the nearest hospital, I realised with mounting anger, that the rogues inside had been watching us all along. They had been silently biding their time till we got within their targeting range. This also meant that the goons were right there on the ground floor, just as my informer had thought. *Advantage Dolas*, my mind screamed in silent fury. For at that vulnerable moment, we were right there in the open, with no shield whatsoever between us and our hidden fugitives. The time was around 1.40 p.m.

My men were forced to take cover till further reinforcements arrived, keeping eagle eyes pinned on the entrance to the building. As soon as the support team arrived, “Come on out, with your hands held high. You are surrounded,” yelled the bullhorn. Nothing stirred for a moment. Then, a strategically-positioned machine gun spewed a diabolic rejoinder to our summons for surrender. Now that our strength far outnumbered theirs, we too replied with random shots to accelerate the pressure and literally smoke the quarry out from their den. In the eerie silence between the firing from both sides, every heartbeat on my side of the law unanimously thudded a ‘do-or-die’ resolve that seemed louder than the roars of the sleek machines at our disposal. Horrified neighbours even hid in their bathrooms (we heard later) out of sheer terror, as more glass-panes shattered and the tension spiralled.

Suddenly, a lanky man appeared at the window of a flat on the second storey, waving an automatic rifle and shouting abuses that were more vicious, more venomous than the bullets he showered. In-between the filth he mouthed, his giddy-headed conviction of his invincibility made him yell, "I am Maya Dolas... you can do nothing to me, do you hear? Not a...."

It was a moment at which each one of us mortgaging our lives out there saw red. The thunderous retort of our gunfire made the foul-mouthed maniac duck mid-word. Seconds later, yet another clattering gun appeared at the window. This time too, our angry weapons roared back. The firing stopped abruptly. An uneasy silence followed. Was it 'two down' or just one missed and the other badly injured? We did not know. All we knew was that we had to, just had to get all of them before this gruesome drama ended. Emerson has said "Even if one life breathes easier because you have lived, that is to have succeeded." I knew how many people would heave a huge sigh of relief if devil-may-care extortionists like these desperados stepped out of their lives. That awareness made nerve-wracking operations like this one worth every drop of the blood and sweat shed to make it successful.

Slowly, very slowly, my men started inching their way towards the building. All roads to the area had been sealed off and the tyres of the crooks' cars punctured, making a getaway impossible. But the men inside did not know that. Nor did they know we now had about two hundred policemen surrounding the hideout. So when two of the gangsters rushed out with blazing guns in an attempt to reach one of the cars, they were killed in an instant. Meanwhile, Maya and another of his feared accomplices had climbed on to the terrace and were firing at the police from behind a tank up there. We decided to split forces. While some of my men stormed into the building from below, the rest of us would try to reach the terrace from a neighbouring building.

The closely-spaced buildings at the Lokhandwala complex proved to be a boon. But there still was a gap of several metres between the top of the building and the adjoining terrace. Many professionals in 'high places' swear that stress actually gives them extra energy, that their adrenaline surges when they are hurtling towards a rapidly approaching deadline. I agree with them. For, not in my wildest dreams could I have imagined that I would instruct my boys to fetch planks from a construction site nearby, and then use these as a makeshift bridge so that we could sprint across the chasm between those two buildings (without looking down!).

You can do what you have to do, and sometimes
you can do it even better than you think you can.
Jimmy Carter

Dolas and Buwa had vanished from the terrace by the time we reached there. But now, there was no looking back. Fired by urgency, we thundered down the staircase. We got Buwa on the third floor and Maya on the first. Meanwhile, the other three, who had hidden in a ground-floor flat, tried to rush out of the side entrance towards the other car. By then, however, it was far too late. The gangsters were totally submerged under an avalanche of bullets from our men in waiting, below. At about 5.30 p.m., a good four and a half hours after I had received that hot tip, the war was finally over.

As the bodies were hauled, one after another, into the police hearse, our jangled and benumbed senses could not initially register the fact that the ordeal had ended. All the seven members of this evil group, which had gathered in a respectable locality, with extortion, kidnapping, and murder on their minds, had a black record of at least thirty to forty offences. Hearty handshakes all around, a warm hug here, an applauding pat there, did a lot to bring our breathing back to normal, to uplift our spirits, to let the horror of the past few hours give way to a happy flood of awareness that we had achieved what we set out to do. True, corruption is like the multi-headed hydra and it was possible that soon enough, seventy or even seven hundred hirelings would replace the seven we had downed. So what? We cannot shirk what needs to be done today or get bogged down by what the day after tomorrow may have in store for us. As long as one carries one's loads with élan, applies oneself earnestly to the present action rather than its future reward, the obstacles in the long race of life will never be insurmountable (Isn't that the essence of the *nishkama karma* that Krishna prescribes for Arjuna on the battlefield in the *Gita*?).

What this triumph did for the morale of the ATS will be clear to you when you know what happened later that very evening. Two of the boys went for a relaxing dinner at a small café in Juhu. As their luck would have it, three troublemakers entered that very joint and asked the manager to "stick 'em up", while they ransacked the cash counter. My boys were in plain clothes and did not even have their personal weapons with them, but who cared? The high that had made their spirits soar because of their success earlier in the day made them pounce on the burglars. Two of the rogues bounded away, but one was caught and handed over to the police van which had been summoned by then. All this convinced people at large that our force could do more than manage traffic or salute politicians! It made them sure that we were capable of handling a fire-fight and emerging as winners. It is only an on-the-spot challenge that sometimes makes you fully aware of your potential, even as it gives your self-confidence a shot in the arm.

However, success and failure, pleasure and pain, bouquets and brickbats, are but two sides of the same coin. How can you truly enjoy an 'up' in life if you have never faced a 'down'? The aftermath of the Lokhandwala operation brought home this indelible truth in more ways than one.

The initial applause was overwhelming. The Chief Minister of the State of Maharashtra, as well as a lot of political bigwigs, called to record their appreciation. We were congratulated, felicitated by the grateful residents, by the Lions, the Rotarians and several other social organisations. Warm letters poured in from unknowns, whose faith in the state machinery and its ability to bring offenders to book had been reinstated. "Congratulations! We are proud of you and happy to know that there still exist such police officers who do their duty loyally, without harming any ordinary citizens. Like Superman, you reach everywhere at the right time and carry out operations successfully. We all wish you great success and a long life!" wrote the president of *'Shakti Mahila Mandal'*, a suburban group working for the empowerment of women. "When honours are bestowed, they're usually well-deserved. Certainly, yours are!" declared another complimentary card.

These reactions from a grateful people more than made up for the trauma of being 'on call' day and night and living from moment to moment, while conducting dangerous operations like the grisly drama at Lokhandwala. Whenever, wherever we were honoured, I told the people repeatedly, that this kind out flushing out of the undesirable elements in society could be possible on a larger scale only if the common man cooperated fully with the men in uniform. "It is only when those of you who know the whereabouts of a miscreant come forward with the information, that we too can live up to the trust you have reposed in us," I said again and again.

Since the entire episode had been witnessed by hundreds of eyes, it was difficult to dismiss it as yet another staged encounter. The entire neighbourhood had heard our loud hailer repeatedly asking the culprits to surrender. Not that this was enough to convince the 'doubting Thomas', though. Two 'honourable' citizens actually filed a writ petition in the High Court, insisting that we had unnecessarily shot down two of the gangsters who actually wanted to surrender. This was dismissed. But the shocking incident was a statement about the magnitude of danger to the common man when unscrupulous extortionists like the Dolas gang set up house in respectable localities.

Lokhandwala suited criminals well because it had a large number of flats bought mainly as an investment by people who lived elsewhere. Many of these owners happily rented out their apartments without always scrutinising the bona fides of the tenant-to-be. This carelessness made it easy for the likes of Dolas to infiltrate these partially-occupied buildings in decent areas. To take every step with caution, to perform every action with awareness is the lesson this story sends out to people who invest in property and then seek to earn an income from it.

At Swati Apartments, Dolas was the key being used by a 'reputed' don to unlock the treasury of many a big builder. The flat was the meeting point where builders were summoned by Maya to pay up or face the consequences. In fact, a rendezvous had been set up for that very afternoon! Are you wondering how we knew that? Well, the phone rang when we were in the flat after our 'Operation Clean-up' was over. One of my men picked up the receiver only to hear someone on an international line trying to find out if the summoned builders had turned up!

Despite the presence of concrete proof, some accusations were hurled at us, even from within the force. The major triumph of the ATS had endorsed our mettle. This appeared to be unsettling for some officers in other long-established divisions, and soon, jealous fangs were bared. What was conveniently ignored was the harsh fact that the ATS did its best without any extra incentives, or even basic protection like bullet-proof jackets and insurance cover. Instead, a few of these debunkers actually implied that, like Dolas or Buwa, we too were on a don's payroll, settling scores on his behalf because some of his goons were getting too big for their boots. Others hinted that it was the builders' lobby which had hired us to finish off the extortionists.

This was pure slander, sheer blasphemy. I wish the deriders had realised what a heavy toll taut nerves take when one has to mastermind a short-notice operation like Lokhandwala with swiftness, composure, and a brand of confidence that can inspire an entire team. I also wish they had taken the time to speak with the four bravehearts from my team who had to nurse injuries to their knees, elbows, lungs. That would have certainly helped them to think twice before questioning our integrity. But then, we had the commissioner and a grateful community on our side to apply salve on our aggrieved dignity. On my part, I requested the state government to reward my boys with some special compensation, and I am glad to report that a total of seven and a half lakh rupees was gifted to them in recognition of their their exemplary courage. Several of my squad members also received bravery medals.

Yet in the final analysis, the truth is that anyone who accepts responsibility for a job that involves human lives stands forever in the dock. That is why, in spite of all the positive reactions we got from the majority of the press, the public, and even the local political party in power, we still had to undergo a trial by fire before the fingers pointing at us were finally put to rest. We had to submit our self-esteem for cross-examination by a special enquiry officer who was appointed to investigate the legitimacy of our actions, and present a detailed report of the Lokhandwala shoot-out.

During the hearing in court however, many senior journalists testified in our favour. Besides, the trump card in our hands was the live coverage of the entire operation by an eminent television news network. Luckily, they had been 'shooting' at a site nearby and had grabbed the opportunity of capturing a hot and exclusive story like this one, live! So both the cases were eventually dismissed, but not without reminding me that however high one may fly on the wings of success, one must always be aware of the possibility of being abruptly pulled back to earth. To give an ironic twist to legal lingo, this case taught me that you are forever guilty, until you are proved innocent. *C'est la vie!*

Be that as it may, the fact remains that at the end of a gruelling day, if you know from within that you have given the assignment in hand your best shot (!), nothing else matters.

CHAPTER EIGHT

MY GUN AND I

No, I never played with guns, never shot down imaginary villains, nor won mock battles when I was a little boy. I was too busy either devouring books, or scampering for runs on the cricket field. Even when I got selected for the IPS, I do not recall being fired with fanciful thoughts of brandishing sleek weapons to make the enemy cower or bolt. Therefore, when our training began and I held a gun for the very first time, I confess I was overwhelmed, though more by a sense of awe than of power. As the realisation slowly dawned that this inanimate tool in my grip could take away another person's right to live, I felt a permanent cloak of responsibility settle about my shoulders. I also felt that my novice judgement had to grow by a few notches before I could extend my hand fully to bond with this potent and perpetual on-job companion!

Since the idea was to initially teach us the basics of handling these instruments, we were given very light rifles – the .22 caliber, or even lighter models. The service rifles used in those days were the cumbersome .303 caliber relics of World War II! But that is beside the point. What is more significant is that not only were our instructors very good, they also succeeded in dinning into us a healthy and lifelong respect for the weapon in our hands.

It is natural for any unarmed and uninitiated man in the street to gasp mentally at the sight of any person carrying firearms, for the visual evokes a cocktail of subdued fear in the mind, spiked with a dash of admiration. What the envious guy cannot fathom is the indelible truth that the disadvantages of possessing a lethal toy like this, far outweigh the glamour it projects or the probable good it can do. For instance, the slightest negligence in handling a loaded gun can sometimes lead to tragedies, unleashing a lifetime of grief, guilt, and a sense of irrevocable loss. There are innumerable horror stories of how a curious child or servant has laid hands on a wrongly-placed weapon, resulting in a fatal accident.

Most lay persons are not temperamentally equipped to carry firearms. For this is not a mobile phone or a digital camera that you can handle with just one-time instructions. You have to exercise a smooth blend of familiarity and restraint in your affair with your gun. Otherwise, you are only asking for big trouble! A gun-owner with a volatile temper, for example, may be easily provoked into misusing it just once, and then finding the rest of his days sucked into the quicksand of a deep and indelible regret. Frankly speaking, there is hardly anything to be said in favour of owning a gun you may never have to take recourse to. Remember also, that even if you have a bulging holster and an ugly crisis staring you in the face, there is absolutely no guarantee that you will be able to muster the split-second spunk needed to use your weapon successfully. That kind of nerve and bull's-eye marksmanship certainly do not come as free gifts with your license.

For police and service personnel however, possessing a gun is obviously an advantage. While sincerely serving the cause of duty, we protectors tend to raise the hackles of many a callous and unsavoury violator of the law. Incurring such enmity and the risks attached are no doubt, part of our portfolio. But sometimes, this can put our lives and those of our families too, in jeopardy. Therefore, keeping a gun at hand does give us an edge over the ill-wishers at large.

Speaking for myself, in spite of the special protection granted to me by virtue of my position and the high-voltage assignments I handled, I always felt safest knowing that my well-oiled machine was at hand, ever ready to take charge of an ugly situation. I remember a reporter of the *Esquire* once asking me skeptically, how I felt safe with a mere pistol to protect me. To date, I stand by what I said to him that day – "My pistol takes eight rounds. If I cannot protect myself with the eight rounds in this magazine, no one else can!"

> *You can get a lot farther with a kind word and a gun, than a kind word alone.*
>
> Al Capone

Have you ever seen and sensed the feeling of security and ease exuded by a blind man being led by a faithful and well-trained guard dog? I cannot think of a better example to illustrate the rapport between me and my gun. For it too has been a mute, trustworthy, and long-standing friend. Any buddy, who offers you unconditional support on a twenty-four-hour basis, deserves your care and concern in return. So it is only natural that I lavish a lot of attention and affection on the instrument that has never failed me when I needed it the most. I sincerely believe that you must take good care of anything that is important and indispensable to you.

In fact, I would extend this to include human relationships too... wife or husband, child or parent, friend or kinsman, one must nurture every tie, stretch all available resources, invest time and effort in strengthening every bond that has added colour to one's life and made it better, more complete, more meaningful. I promise you will never regret your decision. On the contrary, you will reap a bumper harvest of the deep sense of well-being that comes to those who give their very best to life. This is an undisputed law of the universe – when you give without reserve, you receive much more than you think you deserve!

To return to my valued 'accomplice' in tackling crime, a top-rung police officer is, by and large, sheltered from the day-to-day hazards faced by an average citizen, who may have to tackle muggers, petty conmen, or anyone trying to disrupt his normal life. Mainly because the super-cop enjoys perks like an intimidating uniform, a distinctive chauffeur-driven vehicle, the back-up of hordes of policemen who are just a whistle away, and so on. Upon retirement from such a high pedestal, when you are suddenly stripped of all that extra padding, you do feel a bit like Little Boy Blue – kind of displaced, and a little lonely. At such a time, if you have to take a long road journey alone, especially through previously uncharted territory, I cannot overemphasise the confidence triggered by the supportive co-pilot nestling in your pocket.

In spite of being provided with a trained bodyguard, I never had the mindset that would permit me to rely solely on his courage and skill. I always thought: *He is a human being, after all, not a robot. Who can say for sure that he will not lose his nerve and run for cover in an emergency?* Let me put it like this – if you have bought the car of your dreams with your own hard-earned money, would you rely only on your driver to look after it? "No, of course not. It is my car; you cannot expect an employee to feel the same love, the involvement I have with my prized possession," would be your retort, right? That is the whole point; especially when one is talking about the one possession to which only you can claim sole ownership rights – your life! Now you know why I have always preferred to rely on my own gun and my own reflexes to safeguard it.

Yes, the law does grant you the right of self-defence, and if there is imminent danger to your life, killing is not a crime. When face-to-face with a ruthless attacker, being morally strong and legally aware, all you may want to do is to incapacitate him in some way. But the stress and danger may overpower your aim, and a death may result. Such incidents are unfortunate, but if you have only done what you could in order to save your own skin, there is nothing to feel bad about.

I do not have to tell you who won the war.
You know, the artillery did.

Gen. George S. Patton

To prevent ordinary citizens from having to experience such harrowing guilt through no fault of their own, I have often wished the government would encourage the production of less harmful devices for self-protection like pepper-gas sprays, which can deter a rogue quite effectively without causing lifelong or fatal damage. I also feel that a close monitoring of the level of physical fitness, coupled with training in self-defence techniques like the martial arts, should be a compulsory part of the curriculum in all educational institutions.

When I held the reins in the police force, I had made this a 'must' in training programmes for police personnel. A sound foundation in martial arts, imparted by a genuine Sensei, serves a two-fold purpose: you learn to protect yourself and, what is equally important, you also acquire the two all-important qualities of discipline and humility. A perfect teacher of this essentially spiritual technique of honing body and mind, reflex and intuition, will make you a master, and at the same time make you understand why you should never strut around misusing your skill to bully the meek and weak around you.

Come to think of it, in the wrong hands, even a pen can cause more irretrievable harm than a gun. A malicious writer can manipulate this tiny gadget in order to maim someone far beyond the range of visibility. I mean, a writer's mud-slinging antics can tarnish and ruin a reputation, and virtually write someone off without actually snuffing his life out. While everyone knows, and crows about which is mightier, no one insists that you procure a license to own a pen in this mad, mad world!

Real life rarely gives you a second chance to play the same innings. It is also not a glitzy, star-studded game show, where you will always win because you dare. Which is why, whether it is a pen or a gun, the tools of your trade need to be handled with care. Remember what the wise ones say? When the Great Scorer comes to write against your name, He sees not what you lost or won, but how you played the game!

CHAPTER NINE

YOURS UNFAITHFULLY

The main difference between a gangster and a terrorist is that the gangster does not wear rose-tinted glasses. Whether his portfolio comprises collecting petty protection money from illegal vendors, 'lifting' a businessman's child for a hefty ransom, or coolly pumping bullets into an unarmed and totally unprepared X, Y, or Z, the gangster's shrewd mind has only one goal – to make a faster buck, period. So he asks no questions and swallows any lie, so long as his blood money is handed over to him on time. Moreover, being a 'material guy', even as he mouths filth or 'executes' his high-command's orders, his own emotions stay switched off, unruffled.

The terrorist, on the other hand, may spring from humble stock and have only a dull, easy-to-corrupt sensibility. Conversely, he may also hail from the aristocracy and have a super-IQ (the man who killed reputed columnist Daniel Pearl had a degree from the London School of Economics, remember?). Both pedigrees are ideal for manipulation and misuse, as long as the 'lamb' in question does not, will not, think with his head. For only then can his unique brand of naivety be carefully stirred and systematically brainwashed by a 'guru', so that he comes totally under his spell and learns to feel passionately, but with a robotised heart! Blissfully unaware that his emotions have been twisted to mirror the distorted vision of his short-sighted puppeteer, the overgrown kid then walks the wild side with blindfolded bravado until he reaches his 'dead end'.

The big thieves hang the little ones.
Czech Proverb

Yes, he may be paid very handsomely for his obedience. But the biggest coup achieved by the organisation a terrorist-to-be joins, is the manner in which it engraves upon his impressionable mind, the firm conviction that he is *en route* to becoming a martyr to further the cause of his like-minded brethren. Yet another 'perk' for this brainwashed species is the cleverly injected delusion that as soon as each one of these warriors ascend to heaven, their self-denial, their noble sacrifice will earn them an eternal feast of wine, women... in short, every pleasure they willingly forsake on earth.

Both these perfectly-transplanted beliefs (firstly, that this is the uplifting task that every fundamentalist is born for, and secondly, that he will receive divine compensation for it) make the poor blighter feel like the 'chosen one'! Misled thus by insular, communal guides, he moves around brazenly, totally unmindful of the possible dangers to his own life. That is what makes him difficult to break during a cross-examination. That is also why, unlike the opportunistic and objective gangster, the crusading terrorist lives in a permanent state of fanatic intoxication. In fact, this is exactly how the internationally-wanted 'killer for a cause', Manjit Singh, aka Lal Singh, was programmed....

Born in the year 1960, in a small town in the State of Punjab in North India, young Manjit Singh harboured a burning desire to see the wide world. In 1978, as soon as he had passed out of the local school, his strapping physique, nurtured by fresh air and healthy home-cooked food, made it easy for him to get employment doing odd-jobs aboard a cargo ship. For the next eight years, Manjit Singh worked hard and grew more hardy, even as he fulfilled his dream of taking in the sights of many a foreign shore. Then came the fateful 1984, the year of 'Operation Blue Star'.

This highly controversial assignment, given by India's erstwhile Prime Minister Indira Gandhi, saw men in uniform storming the citadel of Sikh faith – the famous Golden Temple of Amritsar, in Punjab. Their mission was to ferret out concealed arms and, more importantly, the men in hiding who were fanning the flames of a growing demand for a separatist Sikh state (Khalistan). Apart from creating international headlines, this militant act of trespassing into a place of worship was decried by outraged Sikhs worldwide, as an act of sacrilege that wounded their religious sentiment and displayed a blatant disregard for the fine line between what is legally and ethically permissible. Radical Sikh youths swore that they would not tolerate this act of disrespect to their faith. Manjit Singh was one of them.

In fact, soon after Blue Star, when his tanker landed at Vancouver, he totally abandoned his seafaring career. Some of the highly placed Sikhs there had convened a meeting at the local gurudwara. Long, motivating sermons were given, and every Sikh was incited to avenge himself against this unpardonable act of the Indian Government. Young and able-bodied men in particular, were made to take oaths that they would abstain from eating meat or drinking any intoxicant, and even lead a celibate life till the formation of Khalistan. Manjit happily quaffed the amrit. He also pledged his unconditional support to 'Mission Revenge'. It was a decision that changed the course of this strapping twenty-four-year-old sailor's life dramatically, and made him rush headlong into troubled waters.

Manjit Singh first attracted police attention on October 31, 1984, when he, along with two other comrades, danced in jubilation and distributed sweets on the streets of New York, to celebrate the assassination of Indira Gandhi. While one of the three soon became the editor of 'Khalistan Times' and the torch-bearer of the Khalistani movement in the US, the other two (including Manjit, then known as Lal Singh Lally) speedily metamorphosed into hardcore terrorists. In November, Manjit joined Camper's 'school for mercenaries' at Birmingham, Alabama. His tuition fee came from the credit card of a supporter of the movement. Some of the exclusive skills taught at this school for rebels were – how to withstand torture during long hours of interrogation, how to survive on bare essentials when in hiding, and so on. Camper's school was in fact an FBI-monitored ploy to keep tabs on the Khalistan promoters in the US, but the rebels-in-training were not aware of this.

Much later, in an interview in Penthouse, Camper described his Indian students as "average", but said that their aims were monstrous in size and intent – they planned to blow up bridges, trains, even atomic reactors in India, and to "be prepared" for Prime Minister Rajiv Gandhi when he arrived in the USA. This assassination plan assigned to Birk failed and he got arrested, while Manjit and Ammand continued to elude the US police. Another plan to "finish off" the chief minister of the North Indian State of Haryana, who was in the US for medical treatment, was also foiled and some more of the revolutionaries nabbed. However, Manjit (alias Lal Singh) managed to escape yet again. The FBI then circulated posters of Lal Singh all over the world. They had facsimiles of his fingerprints and showed him in a variety of disguises. They also declared that he was "wanted" on charges of conspiracy to assassinate a foreign official, and to possess and receive explosives and machine guns.

Manjit and Ammand Singh now surfaced in Vancouver once more, and enlisting the support of the local pro-Khalistanis, planned their biggest sabotage ever. While one booked himself on a flight to Tokyo, the other bought a ticket for Air-India's flight Kanishka, bound for London from Toronto. While neither of the plotters boarded, their luggage containing explosives, was loaded onto the two aircraft. While the Canadian carrier exploded at Narita after all the passengers had disembarked, the unfortunate Kanishka took a fiery plunge into the Atlantic just south of Cork, Ireland, killing everyone on board. Now, the Royal Canadian Mountain Police also put their searchlights on to capture Manjit.

Did the master-planners of these major man-made disasters spare even a single thought for the innocents who paid with their lives, or for the heart-broken families they left behind? Did it ever occur to them that no religion ever prescribes this form of mindless violence? Did they realise that every evolved Master who has assured mankind that the kingdom of heaven is right here on earth has also repeatedly stressed that unadulterated love is the only key that can unlock that kingdom's doors for you? No, they did not. All they wanted was to snuff out innocent lives just to make an absurd show of power, just to arm-twist a country that had hitherto given them equal rights, to now bow to their demands for a separate identity.

A fanatic is a man who does what he thinks the lord would do if he knew the facts of the case.

Finley Peter Dunne

Like all hardcore, blinkered fundamentalist organisations, this one too was demanding the right to play with other peoples' lives, just to create its own illusory Elysium, its own private paradise. Their actions (or for that matter, the tragedy of September 11 and the ongoing killings in the Indian State of Jammu and Kashmir) are all examples of the gargantuan proportions a single seed of hatred can take on. Worse still is the fact that this manic destruction is attributed to the cause of religion and believed to be equal to an act of worship.

Going by the universal belief that man is fashioned in the image of God, perhaps it is natural for him to make even that Supreme Power stoop in order to resemble his own dwarfed sensibility. Quite forgetting that it is only when we remove the cobwebs of selfishness and religious bigotry that the awareness of the underlying unity in all of this glorious diversity will arise. Then, and only then, can the resplendence of the true divinity hidden within each one of us shine forth.

After the 'successful' Kanishka massacre turned Manjit into an overnight hero, he apparently found sanctuary in Pakistan, where he was given a new identity, gifted a palatial bungalow, and enjoyed a luxurious lifestyle. He was also promoted to the rank of 'planner'. He now became a strategist for enlisting more support for the movement and for illegally transporting arms and ammunition to his fanatic fraternity in India. At the time however, our police force in Mumbai was not fully aware of all this. Nor did we know that in November 1991, Manjit had once again set his treacherous foot on native soil, this time as Mohammad Iqbal. A sudden, urgent message one evening from the Intelligence Bureaus of both Delhi and Punjab, therefore, created a big buzz in our office. We were told that Manjit Singh was suspected to be on the Amristar-Dadar Express, which would reach Mumbai in the early hours of the following morning.

As usual, there was a lot to be done and very little time. Hurriedly, we dug out all the FBI notices that had his pictures and fingerprints. The man was by now, a hardened offender and would not be easy to spot. But, knowing the crimes he had already committed and the power he held to create more havoc within the country, we were determined to see that he did not get away.

If you had landed on the platform of Dadar Station at 4 a.m. on that tense morning, you would have nominated each one of my boys for the Oscars, no less! For one was dressed like a porter, another like a snack-vendor, the third was sweeping the platform earnestly. A few ambled around in civvies apparently waiting to receive relatives, a couple of officers togged out in ticket-checkers' uniforms guarded the exit gates, while others hung around outside, posing as eager cabbies waiting to snap up long-distance passengers. Each was affecting nonchalance, yet hovering with a tense heart and a panther's patience, to pounce on this slippery and extremely dangerous traitor.

By the time the train rolled in, our nerves had stretched to the point of snapping. *Is it this one? Or that? Did Manjit actually board the train? Are we really going to pull this off? Or has he already alighted mid-way and evaded arrest once more?* These were some of the questions on everyone's mind as we feverishly scanned the stream of weary travellers who were getting off, assembling their luggage, and heading for the exits.

Just like an experienced head honcho is aware of, and prepared for, all the possible things that can go wrong in a new venture, a veteran terrorist is always on the look-out for concealed captors, or for a police contingent lying in wait for him. We knew that. But we did not know if our man was carrying arms, if he was with accomplices, or how he would react if accosted suddenly. Chances were, he would smell trouble beforehand and just jump off the other side of the train and attempt a getaway. Worse still, was the probability of his firing indiscriminately at the crowd on the platform. But there was nothing we could do just now, except wait and watch with an eagle eye.

People kept spilling out of the many compartments, but there was no sign of the tall, hefty and bearded Sikh we were looking for. Had he got wind of our likely presence and cancelled his trip? Was the information we received incorrect? Or had he donned yet another of his master disguises?

The train was almost empty now and the crowd had also thinned down. Our hopes were plummeting. It really seemed as if something had gone wrong somewhere. I was just yielding to such misgiving, when from my vantage point at the entrance of one of the waiting rooms I spotted a tall, fair, well-built, and clean-shaven man in a safari-suit alighting from one of the compartments. He looked exactly like a successful, touring businessman and was even carrying the typical 'hold-all' briefcase that frequent travellers use. The man began walking unhurriedly towards one of the exits.

Could this be our quarry? Or would we be embarrassing an honest man on a genuine business trip to Mumbai? What should we do? In a couple of minutes the man would vanish through the exit. So, at the risk of committing a *faux pas,* the time to act was now, at this very instant. I quickly made a sign that was passed on by my chain of men. Meanwhile, my officers at the exit point 'Mr. Safari-suit' was heading for, had also been eyeing him with suspicion, because most of the passengers had dispersed by then and there was no one else as tall, or broad-shouldered in sight. Besides, years of focussed and agile policing (or any other kind of work, for that matter) always sharpen your sixth sense, your intuition, your gut feeling about something or someone. It pays to listen to this inner voice. So mutually, but wordlessly, we decided to take a chance.

Four squad members pounced on the man as soon as he crossed the turnstile at the gate, pinning him to the ground while his briefcase just flew out of his fingers. Even as he yelled in protest and struggled to get out of our clutches, one of his hands was heading for the pocket of his suit. My man pre-empted this and waded through its expanse to find a cyanide capsule, the classic 'last resort' of a terrorist when he thinks all is lost. This was tangible proof that our captive was neither an ordinary tourist, nor a travelling businessman; that he was indeed, the man we were looking for. Yet all through the scuffle, he kept repeating that he was 'Mr. Khanna', and that we would all be taken to task for manhandling him thus. But we were not going to buy that. We soon bundled that huge frame into our van and headed back to the office, to launch our next trial – of making Manjit spill the beans about his true identity, his motives, his international connections, and his many misdeeds.

Troubleshooting, or sourcing the root cause of a problem that is having multiple, negative repercussions at the workplace (or even within your own personality), only means that you have just taken the first step towards finding a solution. One has to now begin to work out all the possible ways and means of uprooting that cause, of eradicating it forever. While the initial stage may seem difficult, this one is definitely the more arduous, for it needs a huge amount of confidence, composure, alertness, and restraint. This is what we discovered when we returned to the office with our 'prize catch' and began the long and laborious process of trying to make Manjit talk.

Believe me, compared with what we had to go through on that day to loosen his tongue, the heady moment of his capture actually started to seem insignificant! You can 'melt' a man with a petty, short-term goal easily by simply throwing a couple of threats in his direction. But how do you soften a man who is more than willing to lay down his life for his cause, who would have happily swallowed the poison pill and bid *adieu* to life, but for our timely prevention?

The Indian police force has some officers who are excellent interrogators. My ATS too, had its share of men whose skill in drawing out a sullen and uncooperative criminal was *par excellence*. But even they had to try for a long, long time before Manjit even opened his mouth. As per our strategy, each of the officers was allotted an hour, and each one asked him the same questions again and again. Some would use a rude approach, like calling him a "coward" for running away after committing mass murders, while others would be more gentle and complimentary about his faith, his fervour, his extraordinary commitment. This was done exactly in the 'good cop, bad cop' style that you must have read about either in the papers or in 'whodunit' paperbacks.

For some inexplicable reason, just when we were about to throw up our hands and call it a day, Manjit suddenly responded to the queries of one of my exceptionally skilled boys. His natural manner of exuding both calm and concern must have somehow touched a chord in this once-rustic boy with a wholesome, caring upbringing. The exact time when he finally 'broke' was 5 p.m. For all of us still stuck in the office, that historic working day had begun much before dawn, but who cared? Patience and perseverance had paid off, our captive bird was willing to talk, and that was all that mattered!

Once he opened up, I was amazed to find that for all his dark deeds, Manjit was quite guileless and unsophisticated at heart. In fact, he even told us that if we had resorted to just beating the daylights out of him, we would have never succeeded in opening his sealed lips. Once he had been won over, Manjit gave us the names and telephone numbers of his contacts in Lahore, New York, and London, who regularly sent him funds for the (Khalistan) movement. Our efforts to ring two of them were unsuccessful. This is because the unwritten rule in 'subterfuge networking' is that if your link does not ring you at the appointed hour, it means there has been a glitch of sorts, so you cut off communication till the comrade surfaces and sends out a fresh feeler through a different route. But the third guy Manjit mentioned actually lifted the receiver, smelt a rat, and then hung up abruptly, saying, "There's no one of that name here."

Manjit also told us how camels without attendants were trained by terrorists to transport illegal arms across the Kutch border (the desert region to the north-west of India). These sand-coloured ships of the desert had mastered the art of carrying goods from point 'A' to 'B'. Not just that, they would also virtually 'melt into the sand' at the slightest noise – whether it was of an approaching vehicle, or the whirr of a propeller overhead. Manjit then gave us the name of the man at the Gujarat State check-post who received the goods or allowed the arms-consignments to pass 'unseen'. Very conveniently, the man also owned a *dhaba* (wayside snack joint) at the spot, and this must have doubled up as a storage-bin too! We shared all this information with the CBI (the Central Bureau of Investigation) when they arrived on the scene. But that was later. At the moment, as Manjit educated us on his modus operandi, I could not help thinking, *Who says you can learn the tricks of the trade only from helpful colleagues or superiors? Sometimes, an opponent trying to outwit you can be an unwitting teacher too!*

The biggest scoop we got from Manjit was about a huge stock of arms tucked away in two flats in the city of Ahmedabad in Gujarat State. The haul, as it turned out, was worth a cool four-crore rupees! Other tips from him helped the CBI to arrest a number of sympathisers of the movement. The CBI comes in whenever offences are committed by the same group in more than one state. We were able to give them the exact names of influential Sikhs who were organising camps to lure gullible young men, and also of the riot-instigators from Punjab in the west to Bengal in the east. Are you beginning to comprehend what a trump-card Manjit alias Lal Singh proved to be?

My ATS had nabbed so many hardcore criminals from the underworld before this drama at Dadar. But we had always seen that while the gangster thrives on the fear he creates in the hearts of the people he threatens or lords over, if you succeed in cornering him alone, you discover that he is a pitiable coward. Whereas we could not help feeling a sneaking admiration for offenders like Manjit, because of their total and absolute commitment to their cause. This utter disregard for personal safety, combined with their courage and tremendous skill in handling weapons and technical equipment, makes them much more dangerous opponents, whether they clamour for Khalistan or belong to the Taliban.

It is natural and normal to expect applause, compliments, some perks, a couple of 'bonus points' when you complete the task assigned to you to the satisfaction of your superiors. But, if you think that the successful capture of a globally-wanted offender like Manjit Singh brought us national acclaim and international glory, you can think again. Three weeks after he had been nabbed, the CBI took him to Delhi and then to Ludhiana and Aligarh, after which, believe it or not, we lost track of his fate. The bald truth is that the CBI did not even have the courtesy to inform us what the end result was. This is a major problem prevailing not just in the police or investigation departments, but in most government agencies. In fact, I can extend this further and state that the desire for one-upmanship, the craving to hog the limelight alone, the plotting behind an associate's back, is a deadly virus that maims and eventually destroys any group or groups working towards a common goal, whether good or bad. This is tragic, but true.

However, for any individual who realises that the world is his or her classroom, and who believes in constantly aiming for excellence, this kind of repeated frustration is an invaluable training ground. For you to contribute your best to whatever task you have chosen to do, not for applause, but for an approving nod from the censor within. You learn to aim for perfection as an end in itself, rather than as a means to an end. Every moment, everyday, you try to stay anchored in peace even as you faithfully, meticulously don your personal armour of skills and strategies and go to war.

CHAPTER TEN

A REWARDING PUNISHMENT

Have you ever tried to smash a fist into a stone-cold wall? Or sat hollow-eyed in the dead of the night, clutching onto a plummeting self-esteem, hating the snoring world and praying that the sun never wakes up? Or felt handcuffed without metal and caged without bars? If the answer is yes, then you know how it feels to be manoeuvred by forces beyond your control and to be marooned beyond the shores of reason and justice. The worst part of this reality is that such gargantuan shifts of status have incredibly innocuous beginnings.

> *Accept that some days you're the pigeon, and some days you're the statue.*
>
> Dilbert

Here I was, merrily in the saddle as Deputy Commissioner of Police, Mumbai, when a casual phone call landed me at the wrong time in the wrong place and unleashed a chain of events that turned my world upside down. Just like that. When a dear friend rang me around noon one evening, all he wanted to know was if I could help his ailing father to get inside the airport to meet his *guru* – the Ismaili leader Aga Khan – who was passing through the city that night. The morning had been uneventful, my bounce was in place, there was not a blemish on my horizon, and I was in a mood to play the Good Samaritan. So I volunteered to drive across the city and escort the old boy into the VIP lounge myself. No harm if you stretch your day a bit to gift a dad with tired bones an immortal moment... or so I thought.

Mission accomplished, I was on my way out of the airport when I heard a commotion behind me. Turning back, I saw this man in *khadi* going purple in the face as he yelled at a cop standing before him, while the crowd around swelled. Getting closer, I gathered what the ruckus was all about. The VIP was livid because the police inspector had denied him permission to go right up to the tarmac to meet the chief of a political party. A willful flouting of rules does not become a lesser offence just because it has been committed by a 'bigger' man, does it? So I walked up to the furious bigwig and told him that abusing an officer who is performing his duty is wrong.

"I see. So? Are you going to arrest me for my crime?" the troublemaker sneered.

This kind of blatant arrogance never fails to ignite my blood. "Of course I will," I retorted and proceeded to do exactly that. Four of the officers on airport duty were asked to shift the cocky heavyweight manually to the police van and then to the lock-up, where he had to cool his heels awhile before being bailed out. However, while the 'man of the people' conveniently failed to remember why he had been nabbed, he did not forget who had brought him to book.

As soon as the forever-fickle political tide turned, first making this offender the deputy chief minister and then the home minister of the state, his vengeful axe struck. It happened one midnight! I was served transfer orders, asked to hand over charge, and proceed immediately to Jalna, a sleepy district in the interior of Maharashtra, to take up the post of commandant of the Armed Forces Battalion stationed there. However hardened, however aware one might be of life's capacity to deliver an unexpected blow, one still feels stunned and temporarily unhinged when the delivery hits exactly where it hurts.

At first, I just could not believe this had happened to me. I did not think I deserved this 'shunting out' as it were, just because I had done the right thing to the 'wrong' man. What I had obviously not taken into account was that a person who had shouted down an officer doing his job even when his political party was not in power, would make a much bigger and uglier adversary once he occupied a throne of unlimited power.

Who says an evil mind cannot chalk out a perfect plan? The strategy of a schemer can, at times, shock you by the accuracy and efficacy of its negative focus. In my case, this vengeful man actually took the trouble to interrogate some boot-licking 'fawns' among my colleagues in the force. This is how he found out which place I would dislike the most, before banishing me like the kings of yore did when they wanted to teach a lesson to someone they felt threatened or humiliated by.

I confess my normal 'pep' was dysfunctional when I arrived, with my bags and baggage of magnified hurt and indignation, at Jalna. Victimisation of this kind can play havoc with your morale and numb the fighter in you for a while. So I sulked around for a few days pretending this was a bad dream, conning myself that a miracle would transport me back to my high saddle in Mumbai. All through this ugly transition period, I was totally unmindful of what effect my bizarre behaviour was having on the new men under my command.

What I did not fully realise at the time, was the incredible and indelible fact that hidden within this petty identity of name and form in each of us, travelling with it on the highs and lows, the ups and downs of the demanding and often dizzying rides of life's amusement park, is a Greater Self that remains forever untainted, unchanged, and unvanquished. A friend for life, this eternal witness watches you from the wings, prompts your lines, shields your flaws, and softly but surely, eggs you on to do better and better.

I do not think there is anyone else in the whole wide world as supportive, or more patient. Let me explain. When you ride a wave of triumph, when you are busy accepting the accolades, or reeling under the ecstatic ring of applause for a job well done, you rarely acknowledge its presence. For at that pride-filled moment, it is

'I-me-myself' all the way. You cannot, will not, do not think you owe a speck of this bounty, this glory, to any other source but your own special skills, your own exclusive intelligence. At such power-pointed pinnacles, that inner guide waits quietly, loyally, unmindful of your ignorance of its role in your success.

Suddenly, your giddy-headed climb takes a nosedive and your affair with your preening identity is over. You fall, you hurt... and you feel so alone, so cut off from all things bright and beautiful. The nightmare seems to last forever. Till you accept that you were zooming around with your eyes wide shut. Till you wake up and shake off the cobwebs of self-pity. Till you let go of your crippling 'ego' (which is little more than an apt acronym for 'Edging God Out'). Till you finally let your acknowledgement of that higher power blaze forth. It is this glow of recognition – of the bigger picture, of a greater purpose than obsessing about one's personal goals or grievances – that truly rejuvenates body and mind and renews the resolve to give of your best to whatever needs to be done, wherever you are positioned.

The instant this awareness flooded through my consciousness, my entire perspective changed. Tossed out of the sticky sand of abject self-pity, my cleared head began to tingle with the possible projects that could kindle fresh vigour into this slightly disillusioned and de-motivated battalion. It was time to step out of one's grumpy little self. It was time to don the mantle of responsibilities every group leader has towards his team. It was time for ACTION!

What followed that moment of awakening was one of the most joyful and educative periods of my life in service. I must tell you that generally, the men in any armed police battalion are rough-cut toughs, simple at heart and totally unsoiled by the wiles many of their city brethren acquire (the 'image' they create to court the press and public). As soon as such a band of simple but hardy men realises that you genuinely care for their well-being and are keen to do something to better their lives, you earn their unwavering obedience and devotion.

Whoever you are in the empire outside your threshold, you must admit that all said and done, home is where the heart is. It is in this retreat that you nurse your wounds, or nurture dreams to conquer the world. To quote a universal truth, just like a healthy mind functions only in a healthy body, peak performance on the field is more likely when a man has decent 'digs' to step out from.

Now the standard, age-old explanation for providing drab, asbestos-roofed accommodation for armed battalions like this one was shortage of funds. But when you are determined to find a solution to a problem, you shoot down every excuse that comes your way. So we decided – if the powers that be cannot gift the battalion the homes they deserve, we will override our frustration and access the skills within the group to build our own homes. We quickly made a checklist of our resource bank and found there were trained artisans, masons, bricklayers, carpenters, and electricians in the battalion itself.

True, there was no money to buy bricks, but there was a river-bed nearby. While we used our trucks to transport the soil to the construction site, two potters actually taught us how to design the moulds and make the bricks. Can you visualise the hectic activity that resulted as we set up our own brick factory? Or the energy that passed through hands lovingly designing bricks that would layer their own cozy nests? Never in police history must a drill have been more productive, or as fulfilling.

Our brick-production was so high that we were able to trade fifty percent of the output for cement. The novel enterprise made headlines and my men were thrilled to see a full-page story in a leading daily, on their labour of love. At the end of the collective exercise, we had coarser palms, but bursting hearts and a hundred and fifty handmade homes for an overwhelmed battalion.

What is so awesome about the human spirit is that it forever seeks new obstacles to surmount, bigger challenges to meet, better goals to strive for. As soon as the boys were ensconced in more comfortable nests, they were eager to launch a fresh enterprise. Dipping into the meagre welfare fund, we now started a dairy farm, utilising the land allotted by the government to the State Reserve Police. The produce of this thriving small-scale industry was supplied to the police homes at subsidised rates, while the rest was sold in the market for a sizeable profit. Soon, we also activated a *gobar-gas* plant, fuelled by the manure obtained from the seventy-odd cattle we had bought. This project was financed totally by the *Khadi Gramudyog* (the Handloom and Village Industries Board), and okayed by the local *panchayat* (village council) as part of their efforts to teach villagers to recycle cattle waste.

Thanks to this venture, the homes of the battalion got cooking gas almost free! Now there was no stopping the boys. For instance, once, when the water supply was scarce, off they went looking for water diviners (these amazing people possess the uncanny gift of telling you the exact location of a water-source, by just tapping the surface land with a staff!). Needless to add, we had soon dug our own wells and eliminated the shortage.

When the water supply became plentiful, many of the twelve hundred-odd members of this battalion wanted to create their own plantations. The landscape soon became a lush green paradise where banana, sugarcane, even cash crops flourished. Meanwhile, the profit made by the dairy products went into the Police Welfare kitty, and this was utilised for the books and school fees of the children of these policemen. Can you understand now why this turned out to be the most delightful phase of my career?

This is where I learned to surrender, to trust the master-plan of a higher power, call it God or what you may. Smarting with the insult of being pushed out of sight, to do what seemed like an insignificant job in an inconspicuous place, I had been completely blinded for a while. The last thing that would have occurred to me at the time was the happy possibility of being something I had never been, or learning something I had never imagined I could. In that disheartened state, I had prayed for what I wanted, but (thank God) I had received what I needed... and that made all the difference!

In fact later on, after returning to Mumbai, when I used an armed battalion as a back-up force to quell communal riots, I no longer dismissed them as the dumb hicks that city-slickers tend to take them for. Ignorance may be bliss, but it can also make your vision jaundiced and your judgement faulty. Today, thanks to my 'deportation', I knew both the strengths and weaknesses of these hardy boys. Most of all, I knew how capable they were of giving abundant affection and respect to someone who treats them like human beings rather than faceless hunks of meat to be herded and utilised, or ignored at will.

In fact, looking back, I thank the irate politician who thought he had done a clever bit of arm-twisting by packing me off from Mumbai. But for his conniving malice, I would have never landed in Jalna... and but for Jalna, I would have never known the abiding joy and dreamless slumber that come as a bonus to people who toil with their hands and bond as a single unit, race and religion no bar. I would have never known how many bright surprises illuminate your journey when you walk down a road less travelled by....

CHAPTER ELEVEN

MAY THE FORCE BE WITH YOU

One of the biggest handicaps of the Indian police force is that it is continuously maligned, distrusted, and even ridiculed by such a froth-and-bubble vehicle as the mainstream cinema. This derogatory attitude certainly does not create a healthy climate for the police (or anyone, for that matter) to function in. Your 'peacekeepers' are as much a part of society as you are, are they not?

More importantly, you need them all the time. A petty burglary, a gruesome murder, a sudden riot, an enraged or uncontrollable mob thronging the streets or squatting on railway tracks.... Can any man from the street or even a group of educated and responsible persons, who may be well-meaning but have neither the training nor legal power, ever handle such untoward circumstances that keep besieging normal life? No, they cannot. So one has to turn to these men in uniform to tackle any tricky situation that poses a threat to calm, so that the offenders are nabbed, the panic is dissolved, and normalcy is restored as soon as possible. This gargantuan task can be performed successfully by the force only when it gets sufficient help and cooperation from society, because no successful investigations can be done in a vacuum. This is why a strong bond of mutual understanding between the police and the public at large is essential.

I have a grandson with a mind of his own. Right from the time that he was a toddler, I have noticed that he listens to me only when I listen to him. Closely observing little Mikhail when he is alone or with his playmates, I have learnt home truths that I did not have the time to pick up when my own sons were small. I have learnt that we adults are not the sole proprietors of sentiments like dignity or self-respect. In a world of nuclear families where children no longer grow up as part of 'a herd' of kids that the extended family unit normally reared, a child's sense of individuality and self-importance is sharpened at a very young age.

Today, blind obedience, in deference to a parent or an elder, is hopelessly outdated. On the contrary, if you want to inculcate good values in a child, you have to respect his fundamental right to question your motives, and also (this one is sticky!) to monitor your moves and make sure you practise what you preach. One rash word or wrong move will find you staring at an aggrieved kid with an injured ego and an enormous sulk that may last for days. Yes, we live in a time when the extreme focus on one's own identity and needs makes even relationships nurtured carefully, over specially allotted segments of quality time, tread on shaky ground. In such an environment, how on earth can you demand unflinching loyalty, incorruptibility, and stellar service from a force which you depend upon, and yet ceaselessly deride? Forget the entire police contingent or my thinking grandson. Even a single limb from the body you walk around in, will not support you for long without creaking or complaining if you do not give it the loving care and maintenance it deserves for performing its duties day in and day out. Are you beginning to see that you owe the force something as well?

One indelible fact that the policeman has to make peace with is that his uniform and functions set him apart, make him more visible, so to speak. Thus, while many indolent, or inefficient, or infuriating officials in other departments of government can make life hell for you without making headlines, the smallest error or misdemeanour of a cop comes under the constant and harsh scrutiny of press and public alike. Any slip made by a cop can get magnified out of proportion. While films invariably project the police as clowns or conniving accomplices consorting with criminals, the print and audio-visual media gleefully grab any titbit about a commissioner's posting or transfer and weave endless controversies around it.

All of this is absolutely detrimental to the morale of the police force. In spite of being in a position that is as vulnerable as it is responsible, the regard that is normally accorded to persons in authority is almost never enjoyed by them. As a result, all the good work that the police do is simply taken for granted, brushed off by disdainful rhetoric like "After all, they are getting paid for it, are they not?" An opinion which is as empty-headed as that of a twenty-first century yuppie who yells "You brought me onto this planet, man, so what's the big deal if you had to slave and save to bring me up as well?"

If you see how a cop abroad throws his weight around, you will certainly feel more appreciative of your local *Sakharam* (as the Mumbai slang terms him). I have seen how high-handedly policemen rifled through women's handbags or screened people before entering the stadium grounds at a cricket match in Sharjah. I have heard how rude they can be when they haul you up for speeding in Hong Kong, China or the United States. That is because most of the time no one dares lift a finger at them. Why, even in a small country like Sri Lanka, where I saw quite a few cops who were both physically unfit and ill-trained, I found that the public looks at them with awe.

More than a decade ago, I was at this tiny hair-cutting salon in the Queen's area in New York, when I read about the funeral of a local don who had died in a shoot-out between two rival gangs. The report described how his mafia kinsmen had come in their limos, all dressed in solemn black, to pay their respects to the dear departed. "Can kingpins of the underworld actually walk the streets so brazenly?" I asked my stylist in utter disbelief. "Everyone is hand in glove with them, sir. No one dares to criticise the cops out here," was his reply. If the same scene were to be replayed in Mumbai, we would have swooped upon the mourners and wiped them out, that's for sure. But sadly, few people would have stood up to thank us for sticking our necks out to rid society of such scum... that's for sure too!

En route to USA, I once happened to stop over in London, on the day of Princess Diana's funeral. Since the star-crossed lady had quite a fan following, her untimely demise brought thousands out on the streets to watch the ceremonial procession of the cortege and bid goodbye to their favourite royal. That is where I overheard the remark that the British police were grossly overworked. The words brought a wry smile to my lips. I thought of my men back in Mumbai controlling sixty to seventy thousand-strong crowds with aplomb, working even as long as sixteen to twenty hours on almost every other day. Religious festivities of every community, popular film stars shooting a scene in public, a political rally, consumer protest, communal ill-will, elections, any reason is good enough for the sea of Indian humanity to throng the streets and strain at the leash of the average cop's physical strength and mental forbearance.

In spite of all this, you rarely find a situation getting completely out of hand. Even on jam-packed roads, you rarely hear of a total traffic breakdown in a metropolis. Add to this the occasional firefighting the man on the ground has to do, to keep rock-pelting or barricade-breaking mobs at bay, and you know that the term 'overworked' is part and parcel of his resumé. If the police in the West had to face all this on a non-stop basis as our guys do, they would either resign *en masse*, or ask for reinforcements from the National Guards or simply crack up and make many a therapist wealthier!

"The Italian police are the best dressed and the least efficient," was the verdict of a friend who was on a UNO posting at Rome. He told me how the Mercedes of an African diplomat, staying next door in the Diplomatic Enclave, had been filched in broad daylight. When the frazzled man lodged a complaint, all that he received was a reprimand for not availing of the basement parking facility allotted to him.

The Swiss police do have a better reputation, but truly speaking, my encounter with them was not pleasant at all. My wife and I were at the transit desk in Zurich airport when she discovered that the purse, which contained our passports and tickets for the flight we were to board, was missing. You can imagine the consternation with which we rushed around trying to locate the police cabin on the premises. But when we did get there, all we got was a curt admonition that this was the airline's problem and not theirs, while the door actually slammed on our incredulous faces. The air hostess of our previous flight did find the purse and we finally retrieved it from the counter where she had left it, but that has done nothing to erase the painful memory of the shabby treatment meted out to us by my co-professionals, so to speak.

This is not to say that there are no helpful or praiseworthy policemen in the world out there. All I want to point out is that in spite of all these unsavoury happenings, their cops still command a lot of respect that is dismally lacking in our country. I accept the fact that the average policeman in the UK, USA, Australia, or New Zealand is generally better educated than his Indian counterpart, but then he also makes more money than an officer in an Indian bank. Therefore, expecting that level of education in our men is bizarre when you look at the pay or working conditions we offer them. While choosing candidates for the higher posts is done through competitive exams, recruitment for the lower rungs poses problems mainly because of the bleak prospects this often hazardous career has in store. Obviously, many of those who are not able to compete for jobs with better remuneration end up as policemen. Going by the universal truth that what goes around, comes around, I am of the firm opinion that, in the final analysis, you get what you deserve, whether it is a police force, or anything else.

Take a maid, or a valet, or a gardener, or a chauffeur. These are people many of us cannot do without. But have we honestly ever paused to realise that there is a heart capable of feeling hurt or cheated under those economy-class clothes, or beneath that smart uniform? Granted, there are times when you need to pull them up, or point out that they are not applying themselves fully to what needs to be done. But do you, at other moments, also praise them for a job well done? Or reward them for simply being there, at your beck and call, come rain or shine? Do you inquire about the welfare of their families? Do you know whether they have any chronic health problems, or a major worry that is eating away at their insides as they rush around at your bidding or jump out to open your car door for you? If all you do, apart from handing out their salary, is malign the very people you depend upon all through the day, you cannot build a lasting rapport with them and they cannot give of their best to you.

The same indifference and contempt has demoralised the police in India, where almost everyone considers them to be a bumbling, stumbling, corrupt lot, with no thought about how indispensable they are. Just think of the chaos that would erupt if they were to withdraw even for a single day! Although Indian politics has exposed many a Watergate, the greedy politicians, who have been actually caught red-handed when breaking trust and swindling the entire nation of hard-earned millions, do not seem to kindle as much public ire as a lowly cop does when he stretches out his palm for a couple of hundreds.

While handling enquiries in the Anti-Corruption Bureau, I had once come upon an incredible scam in the Public Works Department, where huge amounts had exchanged hands for the material, labour, and successful completion of a road that never saw the light of day! But such scandals die a speedy death, perhaps because the crimes are committed away from the common man's eye. But the eye can deceive too, and what you see may only be the partial truth. For instance, the highly visible policeman who charges 'extra' at an octroi post may be just the first link of a chain that extends right up to an unseen seat of power.

I will never try to justify corruption. But have you ever acknowledged your own role in making the policeman corrupt or open to making easy money? For instance, if I were to ask any Indian driver who willfully commits a traffic offence whether he prefers to own up and report in court to lawfully pay his penalty, or to speed off after passing on a few bucks, you know as well as I do what his reply will be....

> *The accomplice to the crime of corruption is frequently our own indifference.*
>
> Bess Myerson

Many senior police officers like me have appealed, time and again, to the public to pull up their own socks before damning the force *en masse.* I remember telling a large body of Rotarians, "One of the key elements in the cycle of police corruption is you, the citizen on the street. When you choose a bribe as a detour to evade a fine or prosecution, when you coin a personal 'law' that states 'pay and get your work done', you do not realise that you have set off an amoral chain that can reach alarming proportions. Instead, if you were to complain about a policeman who demands a bribe, you would discover that we have the best machinery for redress, which imposes summary punishments on all those who indulge in corrupt practices. So if you want to set the ball of positive change rolling, you have to change your mind-set first!"

I have often been asked whether the ordinary policeman's lowly income and dismal living conditions are the reasons for his indulgence in corruption. No, I do not think so. Anyone who chooses this profession does so with his eyes open. He comes either because he wants to contribute to the cause of offering protection to the layman, or conversely, because he has not qualified for a better-paying job. I had no expectations of making my fortune in this job. But remuneration is not as important as getting respect for what you do. When that is denied, all the other thorns in this career begin to prick some more. A constantly negative public image is bound to affect the thought process and behaviour of a person. If you repeatedly ridicule someone over whom you have power or control, you are helping to create resentment and a frustrating sense of helplessness, which in turn contributes to germinating the seed of corruption.

What can be even more nerve-wracking is when, just by virtue of being in a job that is forever making news, you become the subject of baseless allegations. You have worked yourself to the bone, done your best for your team and for the greatest good of the largest number, and yet you find yourself hounded or lampooned as corrupt or slack. How do you swallow this? The first human reaction, naturally, is that you hurt. Then, you slowly realise that you are answerable to your superiors, to the court of law, to your government, your near and dear ones, and last, but not the least, to your inner judge – your conscience. If all of them give you a clean chit, you grow a thick skin and turn a blind eye to the irrelevant finger-pointing, period.

It pays to remind oneself again and yet again, that in any arduous trek uphill, there are always more hands willing to pull you down than to heave you up. Especially if you have what it takes to keep treating obstacles as fresh challenges. Especially if your own brand of grit stirs powerful surges of envy in those who have less energy, initiative, and tenacity. Sometimes their vindictive moves can stun you, albeit temporarily. Till your self-confidence rises once more, to point out that mudslinging is the fundamental strategy of the weak and less able.

I remember an incident which occurred when my ATS was doing exemplary work, tracking down hardcore terrorists and trouble-makers. In a suburb of Mumbai, a diabolic duo of two brothers was merrily extorting huge sums of money, not just from builders, but even from people who were redesigning the interiors of their homes! We did not know that these slimy rogues had connections in high places. So when we tried to nab them, we were shocked by the summons we received "for trying to extort money from respected businessmen". How do you like that? It did not seem to matter that the 'respected businessmen' in question had been accused of murder, had a proven record of gold smuggling and links with a gangland don.

When you are faced with a crisis like this, you realise how important it is to have a strong faith that ultimately, truth will triumph. At such moments of trial, even the slightest lack of this conviction can make you dither, make ugly compromises, and then wallow in hidden guilt and shame for the rest of your life. For you may hoodwink the world with some slyly worked out strategy, but there is no getting away from the logbook of the witness within, is there?

So I stood firm by my officers. If I had had something to gain or hide from the minister in question, all I would have had to do was transfer my three men, who were accused, as per his bidding. But I stuck to my guns, my team's morale soared, and ultimately, the case was put to rest.

I must repeat that the portfolio of the Indian police force is far too large for efficient handling. In other countries, specialised agencies deal exclusively with matters pertaining to narcotics, anti-piracy, maintenance of law and order, prevention and detection of crime, and so on. When all of this and more is heaped on a single plate, indigestion is inevitable! Over and above this, the Indian police are also in charge of providing security to VVIPs, ensuring peace prevails in areas prone to communal warfare, and managing crowds at innumerable festivals of different religious groups. No western country places such a tall order or expects so much from its police force.

Today, the amount of government money spent in India on granting subsidies, or fertilisers, or free electricity to farmers is much more than the budget allocation for police welfare, because policing falls under the 'unplanned' category. This is why there is no rationale for the dismal ratio of a constable's earnings to the mounting cost of living, and no explanation as to why a man who works for unnatural hours to protect your home and its inhabitants, should himself be cramped into such atrocious accommodation.

I was once given a temporary posting as commandant of the State Reserve Police battalion. I found that for nearly eighteen years, they had been living in makeshift tents and sheds with tin roofing that gets burning hot in the summer. Yes, the parade ground was lovely and the commandant had a decent office, but in spite of a huge plot being allocated to the battalion, no proposal had been made for the proper accommodation that such a force is entitled to.

It is very important that a reserve police force lives in some seclusion and does not mingle freely with all and sundry, because that can set off unsuitable associations with unlawful elements and affect its efficiency and performance. So the location was perfect, but the facilities to make their lives easier were non-existent. I immediately shot off a proposal demanding their rightful homes, a school, and a hospital. I also received an affirmative reply that the matter will be looked into. But unfortunately, I had to move on before anything was set in motion. Imagine my consternation when twelve whole years later I arrived at the same place, this time as an IGP commanding all the armed battalions, only to find that just a few more sheds had come up in my long absence!

Apart from the miserable fact that no proper housing had been allotted to the contingent, illegal hutment colonies had mushroomed all around the camp. Thus, we had our men staying cheek by jowl with shady characters like bootleggers and petty gangsters, for absolutely no fault of their own. I had argued forcefully on their behalf, and yet nothing had happened. That is the kind of apathy and colossal indifference that our police force has to live with. Now can you blame them if they feel like an unwanted child of society and the government, and therefore, turn a deaf ear to your demands?

Anything that is neglected is bound to decay, whether it is a resplendent plant in bloom, an emotional bond between two people, or a contract between boss and employee. To return to base, a policeman can barely live off the retirement benefits he gets after a lifetime of living on the edge. Unless you are really talented or motivated enough to venture into a fresh line of work, the prospects of a retired policeman are pretty grim. Most of the mediocre ones, who are neither fit and bright, nor adventurous enough to try something new, have a really hard time. Even a top-ranking official, who has been used to certain privileges like fairly good lodgings and transport, finds that he has to change his lifestyle quite drastically to make ends meet. Perhaps this causes some less-ethical cops to stash away whatever they can lay their hands on during the years of service. Greed *is* the root cause of corruption, but let us not overlook the fact that low returns for sincere, day-and-night service can also be a powerful motivator.

Like a young eagle who has lent his plume
To fledge the shaft by which he meets his doom,
See their own feathers pluck'd to wing the dart
Which rank corruption destines for their heart.

Thomas Moore

I feel there is one solution that can arrest corruption in the police force and offer lasting redress to their own grievances as well: the appointment of an independent body or commission that looks after all aspects of managing the police force. Autonomous bodies, totally independent of political control and manoeuvring, should exist in each state and at the centre. They should comprise ten or twelve eminent, socially-conscious persons from all walks of life, like judges, academics, people from the working class, industrialists with a clean reputation, and so on. Some high-ranking police officials may be invited to be consultants, since they have an insider's view of the problems of their tribe. This group should oversee the administration and the financial requirements of the police force, and then rightfully demand that they perform at peak efficiency. Thus, each member of the force would be motivated to give off his best, because he would know that the committee would be striving to improve working conditions and pressing the government to provide sufficient resources for adequate salaries, comfortable homes, education for his children, medical aid, and an attractive take-home package at the end of the month.

There is no other way of eliminating the political interference that keeps making mincemeat of the efficiency or reputations of honest police officials. When morale is high, discipline comes easy. This way, the slightest inclination of the less scrupulous man in uniform to indulge in private gain can also be nipped in the bud by his own immediate colleagues, or superiors, before it takes on epidemic proportions. Most importantly, when the police force is administered by respected members of society, everyone will automatically accord it the regard it has deserved and been denied for a long time.

When the interdependence between any two persons or public bodies is brought home in this fashion, with grace rather than force, with sensitivity rather than tyranny, the mutual respect that results is more real, and therefore, more lasting.

And I am my brother's keeper,
And I will fight his fight,
And speak the word for beast and bird,
Till the world shall set things right.

Ella Wheeler Wilcox

CHAPTER TWELVE

MOB MONSTROSITY

You cannot talk a typhoon out of stomping upon every 'castle' built on sand and galloping out of the desert, leaving behind a devastated, uninterrupted flatness. You cannot stop a tidal wave from turning the sedate world onshore into a macabre water-park, offering somersaults to nowhere. You cannot extinguish the flames of a forest fire by merely showering praises on it. And you cannot bring the raging bull called "mob-mentality" to its knees by merely planting a red banner marked 'Self-destruction Ahead' in its path.

Much as fanatics, fundamentalists, or groupies of any sect, cult, caste, or religion would love to disagree, a mob does not operate on the basis of any rational strategy, or any honourable set of beliefs or ideals. The incident that invites its initial attention may be genuine – a disturbing 'something' that needs to be focussed upon, debated about, and sorted out immediately. But invariably, what provokes the instant follow-on of manic aggression is more of a panic-button reaction, like the blind hysteria of an octopus disturbed on the ocean floor, limbs swaying in frenzied motion. A mob has no religion, no God, except its own headless, mindless, overwhelming ego (an ego that demands attention through destruction!). I know the brute-power of mob psychosis only too well, for I have faced the heat of its blind unreason more than once.

The basic script of every inter-communal scrap is the same, be it a fiery exchange of words between unfriendly neighbours over a bucket of water from the common tap (an everyday phenomenon in the lives of the less-privileged in a metropolis like Mumbai), or a full-blown exchange of gunfire between nations misguidedly employing might to prove that *their* faith is more right. As I said before, the gruesome drama may begin with a single physical or mental wound inflicted by one individual trying to settle a private score, or a group using strong-arm tactics to glorify its stand. But all too soon, when the victimised person or community retaliates, the verbal abuses are replaced by physical blows, flying arms turn into flaming torches, stones metamorphose into crude bombs, and the harsh fumes of mutual ill-will block out the light of reason. Then, hatred couples with blind fury and from this illicit, ill-advised and ill-fated union, a totally unwanted child called 'riot' is born.

The tyranny of a multitude is a multiplied tyranny.

Edmund Burke

Take the winter of 1992. When the Babri Masjid was demolished, the inevitable chain reaction of gouging eye for eye began in Mumbai. First, the Muslims took to the streets damaging the property of the Hindus. Then the backlash began with the Hindus zeroing in on the attackers. Each group turned aggressor in the area where it had a stronger presence. At this juncture, vested interests began to play their own dirty games, inciting violence and committing atrocities in dense slum colonies which could not be adequately policed because of the narrow alleys through which even a two-wheeler could not be manoeuvred. As normalcy creaked to a halt and law and order fled, Mumbai, the fairly safe, progressive, and open-minded metropolis that rewards you for who you are rather than for where you come from, was reduced to a series of bloody street-shows, each more horrifying than the other.

At one suburb, two policemen were killed and dumped into a trash bin. At another, lovingly assembled homes were burnt, women were molested, and the beasts on the streets went on a demoniac stabbing spree. It was as if one of the robotic creatures that sci-fi films fabricate so authentically, had actually come alive and decided to destroy everything in sight. Trying to find out who committed which crime, or whether the larger number of murderers were of this faith or that, was and remains for me a thoroughly pointless exercise, because the truth is – everyone who was out there on the street, brandishing animal instincts and gloating over dubious victories, was guilty.

True faith is all about respect for Creation in all its myriad forms. It is about staunch values, self-restraint, and compassion. None of these exemplary qualities, which reflect the image of God in man, were even remotely visible in the vicious behaviour of any of those two-legged animals stalking the streets during those terrible weeks. Is there any saint, any reformer, any God the world over, who has advised his flock to inflict so much pain and humiliation on another?

When mass violence of this degrading level erupts, the law-keepers are totally overwhelmed, because you just cannot be everywhere all the time! Normally, sending one head constable and three men on the beat to a trouble-spot suffices to quell any dispute that is threatening to get louder. But when there is a mob of hundreds spilling out of every nook and cranny, filling every square and by-lane, all you can do is impose a curfew, pick up the obvious ring-leaders, or just fire in the air to disperse the crowd. We did just that. But, each time we succeeded in creating such a temporary lull in the tempo, yet another gruesome, 'engineered' incident would occur, making the sparks fly all over again. Once, when we thought all was well, two labourers were stabbed. Again, when some patchwork-peace was restored, two homes were set on fire killing some of the inmates. In the third instance, a woman was raped and then burnt to death along with her uncle who went to help her. It truly seemed as if all good sense had fled the earth.

> *There can be no such thing, in law or in morality, as actions forbidden to an individual, but permitted to a mob.*
>
> Ayn Rand

What I would like to stress is that all of this had less to do with the religious affiliations of any of these incensed individuals or groups. But it had a lot to do with their economic and emotional vulnerability, which was being manipulated and exploited by the unseen hands of their fanatic leaders, slumlords, and political aspirants. We Indians know only too well what havoc was wreaked on us by the colonial master puppeteers who slow-poisoned our unity with their crafty 'divide and rule' policy. But, whether it is a struggling individual or a sea of dissimilar people, unless a consistent and determined effort is made to snap the clamps of deep-rooted conditioning, history has a habit of repeating itself.

One set of villains who were happy to keep the riots ablaze, were the local thugs who had captured land illegally to 'rent' it out to poor immigrants drawn to Mumbai in search of a livelihood. When the ongoing trouble made these poor souls flee homewards, the dons were able to make a fresh pile by extracting 'deposits' once again and demanding higher rents from the new tenants. So we started rounding up these crooks.

In those seven weeks that turned the metropolis upside down, I must have gone home barely six or seven times. The rest of the time was spent out on the streets, or holed up in the office. Would any of those marauders have ever understood the fear and anxiety that the blameless children, long-suffering wives, and aged parents of my men in uniform suffered, when they did not come home for days on end? I do not think so. How could they, when they were totally blinded to the long-term repercussions that their impulsive actions were having on their own kith and kin!

My imposition of a curfew in the troubled zones was not looked upon favourably by everyone. Some actually thought I was trying to harass the common man further. This is exactly how the see-saw of life works. Just a few weeks ago I had been a top-of-the-heap hero for gunning down villains who were a threat to civilised society. Now that the insecurity of the current crisis had stretched nerves to breaking point, those very applauders were blacklisting me for my current action.

It takes both conviction and courage to stick to your decision at such moments of trial. But, if your reasons are sound, you can turn a deaf ear to the ranting and stand your ground as I did. At that point of high-pitched tension, there was no other way of arresting the arson. A majority of the troublemakers spilling out onto the streets were unemployed young men. The only way to curb them was by indirectly creating pressure within their homes. Most of these hot-blooded roughnecks had to return to cramped tenements where large families, caged in by the curfew, were fuming as they were unable to go out and fetch provisions needed to keep the home fires burning. You can imagine what a disastrous effect the deprivation of essentials can have on a family of ten or more, which is holed up in a tiny room without adequate lighting or even a private toilet... and worst of all, with nothing constructive to do!

As I had visualised, this naturally resulted in a lot of hardship, prompting the elders to raise their voices and check their boys from stepping out to cause more trouble. They did this in the hope that the curfew would be lifted, but in the process, they also became my 'plants' – my allies living in the very homes of the rioters, sharing their bread and campaigning for restoring peace. No mass arrests, no amount of beating or torture could have achieved this as effectively. The reason is simple – however big his offence, shooting down a person can never have a calming effect on his immediate family. Their first instinct, naturally, is to seek revenge, and so the last thing they are likely to do is to prevent other youths from rushing out to create more chaos.

During a riot or any form of disturbance, when an individual or a group becomes aware of the fact that it is one's own negative thoughts, words, or actions, that envitably boomerang, then one also realises that the first aid for help lies within and not without. It is in situations like these that one needs to rely on cool reasoning, be a little more patient, and trust in the fact that sincere effort to effect positive change never goes to waste. Little steps like these help one appreciate another's point of view as well as understand oneself.

One may even learn, at the risk of some shamefacedness, that a lot of one's self-righteous anger is rooted more in ego than in reasoning. This way, one may have to 'kiss dust' occasionally and admit that one's initial outburst was unwarranted or just plain wrong. However, when arrogance subsides, one may realise that straightforwardness has earned one the respect of those around, and even some in the 'enemy camp'.

About the flak I faced for my firm action against the rioters who continued to go on rampage even after the curfew, let me say that it was an unavoidable part of the game. Most people shun the burden of responsibility that major decision-making in any venture involves, but if things go awry, they are quick to point fingers at the same person who has shouldered the burden of taking charge of a sticky situation. My main concern when the riots were on full-scale, was that the blind violence was putting so many lives at stake, never mind which religion they followed. That is why my ATS men (only one of whom belonged to my faith) stood by me through thick and thin.

That is also why, when allegations were flung at me and cases were filed against me about my 'biased' operations, senior legal experts, whose sense of fair-play overrode all bigotry, defended me in both the lower and high court without even charging me for the expenses incurred. The fact that they did not share my religious beliefs obviously did not come in the way of their regard for me, or their confidence in my integrity. Even the police commissioner of the time, who belonged to the 'opposing' faith in this manipulated 'war of religions', showed implicit trust in my judgement, used me as his right hand to tackle many an ugly episode of a 'fundamental' nature during the riots, and last, but certainly not the least, testified in my favour in court.

I don't think I could have commanded the love and unflinching loyalty of my squad if I had ordered them to illegally down followers of their own faith. I only 'used' my religion once during the riots, and that was when I went to a strife-torn area and requested permission to calm the crazed mob through the public address system of the mosque. I told everyone that this was no way to campaign for justice. I told them to return home, and later, take a delegation to the chief minister or even the prime minister to state their woes and demand redress. I warned them that the police would take severe action if any more public property was destroyed. I also pointed out that by burning buses in Mumbai they could not replace the walls of a faraway masjid they had never even set eyes upon. Instead, all they would do is to ask for an equally senseless bout of revenge that would put their own families in needless peril.

What relieved me most of all, after the riots subsided, was the happy fact that the people went back to their original, amicable 'live and let live' policy which makes Mumbai such a remarkable and much-loved metropolis, to which immigrants throng from all corners of the country. This is a city where a butcher belonging to one religious group supplies animal skins to the tannery run by a man of another faith. Never before has this hindered their working relationship, and hopefully it never will. The fact that that such mass-scale chaos did not repeat itself augers well for the future.

Many individuals in respected positions, regardless of which religion they believed in, supported me whole-heartedly for my sincere peacekeeping attempts. Yet, when I was summarily asked to shift residence to Nagpur, ostensibly to flush out the *naxalites*, I knew I was being punished for a crime I had not committed. This is one of the most difficult lessons in life: to exercise patience when one is most agitated, to keep a tight hold on the reins of impulsiveness when one is most rattled. Not for nothing did the great Milton pen the immortal line: 'They also serve those who only stand and wait'. I had seen incredible highs, enjoyed the sweet thrill of flash-bulbs and fanfare. It was time now to take respite till the indignation cooled and I could think straight again.

But that is another story, another rung altogether on the ladder of personal growth. To return to the issue of man killing man on religious grounds, I have only this to add – when you are sinking in the quicksand of a crisis, you grab any hand that is held out to help. You do not wonder which religion your saviour follows. For instance, if your child is in the intensive care unit and in immediate need of blood, would it matter at all if it came from the arm of someone following a different faith? All disputes on the basis of religion stem either from arrogant overreaction or a deliberate attempt to trigger mob-mania, and thereby divert attention from some other underhand motive which is more rooted in personal gain than in the well-being of the community being manipulated.

Today, thanks to the technological blitzkrieg, we are all part of one global family whose access to instant communication, or instant annihilation, is only a few buttons away. So today, more than ever before, when the whole world is on a red-alert over the same issue of man versus man, we must understand one thing clearly and quickly: If we truly want to uproot the corrupt seed of ugly thinking and imagined differences that is threatening to disfigure, or destroy the entire bounty of the beauteous planet we inhabit, it is high time we asked ourselves, once and for all: *Does one have to blacken another's face to prove one's own is white?* Can shouting oneself hoarse or drawing another's blood to proclaim the greatness of one's own God ever usher lasting tranquillity within? Why then did Mother Nature, from whom all of us draw our sustenance, not turn bigoted, insular, and narrow-minded as well? Why didn't she divide the sky, the sea, or the air that we breathe and distribute it on the basis of our colour, caste, or creed?

CHAPTER THIRTEEN

MY GOD AND I

I am not an atheist. Nor do I believe in using God as a weapon. Or feel that true religion is merely about going to a temple or mosque, or just praying regularly, or rigidly performing some rituals. Faith is a very private, a very personal matter. I do not think anyone outside of your own self has the right to question your beliefs, or to say something like: "How can you say you are a Muslim (or a Hindu, or whatever), when you drink and gamble?"

All the rules telling you "You must do this", or "You can't do that", have been created by religious leaders who like to wield power over people's minds. The entire paraphernalia of ceremony and custom attached to religion is, to my mind, just like the window-dressing that catches your attention and lures you, without giving you a taste of what the inner core of that religion is.

I believe that all those who love their fellow men, regardless of their caste, creed, or religion, are dear to God. Helping a needy human being, or lending a hand to those who are weaker or helpless, is far more important than being fanatical about growing a beard or sticking to a prescribed dress code, just because other people insist that these are the only ways of demonstrating which religion you have inherited by the accident of birth.

If praying five times a day or donating huge sums to places of worship were means to absolve oneself of all sins, then I dare say that some of the most cruel dons and the many henchmen of the underworld would get a cleaner chit than you or I would, on the day of reckoning. Similarly, fanaticism and tolerance are incompatible bedfellows. So whenever and wherever fundamentalism of any kind rears its ugly head, it immediately uses the deadly concrete of deep-rooted hatred and distrust to build walls that divide man from man. Thus creating claustrophobic communes in which the simple abundance of unconditional love can never breathe easy.

Equally despicable is the religious frenzy ignited by political motives. A shrewd contender for a party seat often uses a facile tongue, or a skilled speech-writer to whip up a storm of fanatic sentiment within his constituency. This turns out to be an infallible move, especially if the larger section of the electorate follows the same religion. His reward? A red-hot vote bank and major funding from gullible, but well-heeled sources. Once he settles down on the chair you have eased him into, do you really think he cares about which God you worship? Certainly not. However, each time the chair wobbles and he feels threatened, be sure that he will revert to the same sly strategy of reminding you of your roots and assuring you that he and he alone can be the guardian angel of your faith! This is how religion gets abused and judgement runs askew when manipulated by the twin reins of selfishness and power.

I have never chosen a friend on the basis of whether he frequents a church, temple, or mosque. Perhaps this is because my mother never brought us up as die-hard fundamentalists. At school, college, in the police force, why, even in my ATS, the majority of my close companions and colleagues have been followers of another faith. But that has never created even a wrinkle in our intimacy, or in our smooth, day-to-day functioning.

But then, you cannot expect everyone else to think and feel as you do. So, at a landmark stage in my career, when I felt I was being discriminated against only because of my religion, I turned to the only court of justice where there is no foul play. I turned to God.

This is what moments of crisis have always done for me. They make me introspect. They make me realise that there will always be situations in which you will have no one else around who can truly understand your dilemma, except the Almighty. Yes, it is moments of crisis that make me feel closest to God.

That is when you put aside all the external trappings of name and fame, image and attitude. That is when you approach your innermost, unblemished, and unbiased self, your true source of strength and sustenance. That is when you confess that you are deeply troubled, that you are yet again stumped by the unpredictable, often unjust ways of the world around you. That is when you peel off your ego, go humble, and earnestly ask for help.

"When the solution is simple, God is answering."

Albert Einstein

Talking to God has taught me forbearance. I have learnt to endure what cannot be cured. For instance, after working round the clock to curb the double menace of gangsters and terrorists who had made normal life difficult for the common man, some people actually filed cases against us, saying that we killed criminals in captivity without giving them a fair trial. Now how does one handle a charge like this one? Does one drag the accusers into the heat of battle to show them how it feels to trade bullet for bullet, to live in death's shadow, so to speak? Does one remind them that we have done this day in and day out, not for personal gain but to help them lead a peaceful life? Or does one respond to the court-summons, defend one's honour, and hope for a fair judgement? Choosing the latter option put us 'out of the red' certainly, but apart from a cursory pat from the government in power at the time, it did not fetch my team the laurels or whole-hearted backing we were hoping for. Should one let this crush self-esteem and destroy initiative forever? "No," said God. "Fresh loads usually land on shoulders which are broad enough to carry them. Keep your chin up and your smile on."

Talking to God has renewed my confidence – to rise from the ashes of one failure and explore yet another uncharted territory.

Talking to God has made it easier to accept and love, rather than disapprove and hate.

Talking to God has made me aware of my responsibility of putting to good use, all the advantages I have been given. It has made me work hard, regularly, relentlessly, on keeping myself physically fit and mentally agile – to either face a storm, or to revel in the calm; in other words, to be ready for every moment.

Talking to God has kept me alive!

CHAPTER FOURTEEN

SURRENDER

Watch two children playing a game in which you cannot go solo. They begin quite amicably, each trying to accommodate the other's words and moves, each trying to contribute his, or her own special brand of ingenuity and enthusiasm in a cooperative effort to have a good time. But all too soon, you see the cracks develop; you find the equation getting imbalanced. The one who is either more creative, or as happens in most cases, the one with more brute force and obstinacy, tries to get the upper hand. "NO, not like that, like this!" or, "If I say you are out, you are out, okay?" or worse still, "This is my kit you are playing with, remember?" These are some of the poison-darts the bully employs, more often than not to dispel his own discomfort, which has arisen from the realisation that the 'opponent' is obviously the better player. In a trice, sportsmanship is thrown to the winds. The result is a noisy word-war, or a 'slap-sock-scream' deadlock, calling for adult intervention... while the abandoned racquet, or scrabble-board lies forlorn and forgotten.

Most adults tend to play the same power-game, except that they use more sophisticated vocabulary and more lethal machinery. You may be a sincere worker. You may have given a job your blood, sweat, and toil with utmost diligence, and acquired a prestigious designation solely on your own merit. Many a time, in the process of investing time and patience in your demanding career, you may have let your personal life go askew and returned late, night after night, to an upset family. In spite of this mammoth effort to achieve something spectacular, to get ahead with integrity, you may one day find your superior nonchalantly handing you a ticket to nowhere. All because inadvertently, you trod on the toes of someone who thought you were getting too big for your boots. It happens all the time. I should know. Just as I was planning a little break after what I thought was a job well done, it happened to me.

> *Expecting the world to treat you fairly because you are a good person is a little like expecting the bull not to attack you because you are a vegetarian.*
>
> Dennis Wholey

Out of the blue, I received pack-up orders informing me that I had been appointed chief of the anti-*naxalite* operations at Nagpur with immediate effect. The scene was like an eerie repetition of my previous 'punishment posting' which I had earned by ruffling the feathers of an errant minister-to-be. This time too, there was absolutely no sounding out beforehand, no 'by-your-leave', and certainly no acknowledgement of the fact that the individual being shunted out had invested two and a half dedicated decades of his lifetime, not in just any job, but in a precarious, high-tension post!

You must have read innumerable news reports in Indian dailies of highly placed officers being transferred at short notice by underhand means and for questionable motives. This would never happen if there was a watchdog committee, an All-India Police Commission to whom you could appeal directly if you felt you were being victimised. True, the Central Administrative Tribunal, which functioned semi-judicially, was available for seeking redress. But it got so burdened with petitions that a response to a plea would take as long as five years, during which period, the officer in question could even get re-transferred!

Some years ago, a police commission comprising senior citizens of repute from different walks of life was also created to deal with issues like abrupt postings or transfers. But, sad to say, none of its recommendations were ever accepted by the seat of power. Who will welcome speedy justice, if he knows his own head may roll in the process? The most unfortunate part of this cold reality is that such sudden moves are prompted by selfish interest and not because the grandmaster has the well-being of the public, or the greatest good of the greatest number at heart.

However, if you are a born optimist, or better still, if you work ceaselessly on the obstinate soil of a negative mind till it generates a crop of evergreen hope, you do not let anything or anyone keep you down for too long. Of course you fumble, you stumble, and occasionally even take a tumble (after, all, we all have a right to be human now and then). But, you do not let a temporary fall cripple you for the rest of your days.

You splash new ideas and alternative plans upon your benumbed senses. You go through the physicals of pack, unpack. You placate your spouse and relocate your children in boarding schools, sometimes against their will. You smile your way through all the farewell and welcome parties. You report at your new desk, extend a genuine hand to bond with your new team, even as you force every misgiving into the punching bag in your home-gym, or in upbeat strokes on the badminton court. You also make sure that this relentless 'in-fighting' goes on until the rancour has bolted away, until you have spring-cleaned your insides enough to return to a rational, cool, objective mode again.

That's right.... It is only when you have totally stopped blaming yourself for something beyond your control, only when you have stopped wallowing in the well of self-pity – a well which is only as deep as you dig it – that you can throw away the crutch of clucking supporters. Of course, you do not need that self-defeating sympathy once you have learnt to summon up the deep spring of self-confidence. Remember, it is ever willing to rise at your bidding, provided you burrow far enough. As soon as you have taken a welcome dip in its rejuvenating current, you discover that you can think strong, walk tall once again.

You can now look the capricious chef called destiny in the eye and choose to nod a beaming assent, or wave a graceful hand in rejection of the new course it has ladled out on your life's platter. You and you alone hold the right to take it, or leave it. Once before, when I had been similarly pushed out of sight, I had chosen to take it, and thereby discovered a hidden side of myself that I would have never known otherwise. This time however, after a short span of indecision, I chose to leave it. Let me tell you why....

As far as creature comforts go, my location in Nagpur was impeccable. I could not have asked for more. I was allotted a sprawling bungalow set amidst three or four acres of virgin land. I had the usual retinue of orderlies at home and more than my share of 'yes-men' at work. The only problem was – I also had nothing to do!

After recovering from the initial post-transfer consternation, I had been quite fired up with the thought of facing the new challenge of tackling the fearless *naxals* who were stirring up a lot of trouble by their lightning strikes. But when I arrived in Nagpur I found that the *naxalites*, whom I was supposed to deter or apprehend, operated mainly in the border districts of the State of Maharashtra. Now these areas were located a neat four-hour drive away from where I was stationed. So even when I did get some information about an attack, by the time I rushed there, the troublemakers had enough and more time to vanish into thin air.

The trump card of the *naxalites* is their easy familiarity with the dense forest region that separates Maharashtra from its neighbouring states like Andhra Pradesh or Karnataka. They thrive on shock treatment, meaning, they swoop down on a place, do the intended damage – like 'hitting' a private contractor – and then, literally melt away into the jungle. So, each time, before I reached the spot, they would have already travelled ten to fifteen kilometres to any of the several tribal settlements around. They would then shed their identifiable green uniforms, hide their weapons in a pit or an empty water tank, don the local attire, and begin working at innocent jobs alongside the villagers who kept their lips clamped under threat.

This happened again and again till I realised that in spite of all my positive efforts, the time-gap would perpetually prevent me from doing anything worthwhile. I also realised that the bigwigs who had expelled me from Mumbai had, in all likelihood, transferred me knowingly on this 'mission impossible'.

But for this paucity of purposeful living, I loved Nagpur. I made wonderful friends, there was a lovely badminton court to play endless sets upon, and a huge yard around my home where I grew incredibly green fingers! But for an impossibly hot summer that lasted for about three interminable months, the weather was pretty conducive to gardening, and I soon became the puffed-up parent of four hundred flourishing rose plants. No one could get past me without drooling over them. In the ballistic enthusiasm that followed, I even began planting fruit trees. Then one morning, I rose from the ground, stared at my mud-caked hands, and asked myself: *Is this why I joined the police force?*

"Don't be a fool and quit now. Why lose all the retirement benefits you risked your life for?" "You have done more than enough for one lifetime. Now sit back and enjoy your leisure!" These are two random samples of the well-meaning advice my buddies back in Mumbai had given me when I received my transfer order and wanted to shoot off an inflamed resignation letter. No, they were not wrong. After all, apart from the morass one's bruised ego is flung into by such a 'downsizing', each officer who faces such an ordeal also has the uphill task of first coping with the alienation he himself feels, and then convincing and reassembling his blameless family as well. He also has to keep in mind his responsibility towards securing their future. A hasty, self-centred decision, followed by a lifetime of repentance, is simply out of the question when you have pledged support to lives other than your own.

That bit was fine. After years of doggedly serving the community despite the odds, the last thing I would have wanted to do was to cheat my own near and dear ones of their well-being or peace of mind. My action-packed profession had already put them through enough nail-biting days and sleepless nights. But did this mean I was to spend my remaining six years in service raising an orchard?

As I stood perplexed, head uncovered, in the middle of my garden that summer morning, the sun warmed my limbs and shed new light upon my dilemma. In a flash I knew what I could do, would do, without hurting anyone who depended upon me, and without losing out on what was rightfully due to me from my employers. I would stick it out for another year or so, until I completed the stipulated term of thirty years that would fetch me my full pension and all the benefits due to an officer of my cadre when his term is over. I would then request for voluntary retirement and call it a day.

As soon as I had taken that major decision, I felt a sense of well-being flow back into my heart. No, I did not know which way I would head after going back home. But I knew I could no longer dawdle at a desk signing perfunctory notes, or staring at an unmoving clock. Just as a hungry baby is an unreasonably angry baby, a bored boss is an unpredictable chief to report to. I remember a colleague who was transported in similar fashion, to head an armed forces battalion in a remote area. When the independence of a senior person is suddenly snatched away on a superior's whim, it can unleash mayhem. The 'injured soldier' I am referring to, played such havoc with the boys under him that the whole fiasco culminated in a police mutiny in that unit.

So you see, a mishandled officer can cause much greater damage than a frustrated small-timer, who can vent his anger only on his devoted wife, or bewildered children. The last thing I wanted to do was to make my subordinates pay for the dirty deal someone more powerful had handed out to me. For me, therefore, it was time to change lanes, time to hop off a thirty-year-old saddle and walk alone towards a new horizon.

I never regretted my decision. Yes, I had enjoyed my job for the discipline it taught me, the self-confidence it instilled in me, the responsibilities it planted on me, and most of all, for the sea of humanity that it brought me in contact with. I am absolutely certain that in spite of all its ups and downs, highs and lows, this was the only career that could have brought out the best I had to offer. True, one officer cannot change the system, but he can do a lot to boost the trust of the laypersons reaching out to him, and make them feel more safe and secure. That is all I had wanted to do.

No other profession could have given me the same amount of fulfilment, the same ecstasy on occasion, or on the flip side, the same agony. At the risk of sounding pompous, I must point out that had I acquired a doctorate in poetry instead, I could not have been of vital service to so many people, I could not have done so much for the man on the street. Also, if I had wanted a change after obtaining a doctorate in literature, all I would have found was a dead end!

In spite of how my career in the police force ended, I will always be grateful for the twin lessons it taught me – to be realistic and to be cynical. Those packed years of 'troubleshooting' make you so practical in approach that for ever after, even as you do your best in any field, you stay on red-alert, prepared for the worst, ever-ready to take charge if calamity strikes or if your applecart gets upset without a warning. You learn to look out for yourself without craning your neck to see if help or sympathy is at hand. This brand of alertness-cum-composure proves to be an invaluable asset when you first set foot in the wide world outside to do your own thing, without the cushy support of your official chair.

This is the reason why I never considered putting up a chemical factory or setting up an advertising agency after I got out of the force. I did not want to step into an arena wherein I had neither the know-how, nor the conviction that I could cast correctly to build up an able team. It is better to listen to the horse-sense which warns you that you are more likely to succeed at a business in which you know at least some of the ropes. Thereby, you are more likely to possess better judgement and to hold the reins with an authority that is flavoured with both expertise and awareness. Instead, if you get caught in the fantasy of launching an enterprise that tickles your fancy and lures you with the false promise of glamour and megabucks, you may soon find yourself caught in a nightmare that will not end in a hurry.

One of the areas which interested me, and in which I knew I could contribute effectively, was providing hand-picked and hardy security staff, both armed and unarmed, to individuals, housing societies, private organisations, and industrial houses. This is how my first enterprise, my private and growing army of 'supermen' was born. I was also deeply concerned about piracy and the violation of intellectual property rights. The production of 'fakes' can take an alarming turn when committed in vital areas like edible oils, baby food, and bottled water, affecting quality and causing contamination that can even result in death. I launched a company that would try and keep in check this subtle form of violence that can cause more widespread harm than the most gruesome murder.

Remember, nothing gets wasted as long as you keep your antenna fine-tuned. The trick is to stay open-minded, awake, and alert to the little lessons life keeps teaching you, and also to the innumerable little blessings Lady Luck keeps showering on you. Why, even waking up every morning feeling grateful to be in a fit body, taking in a few breaths of fresh air, doing a few stretches to tone up, zipping out for a short bracing walk, enjoying the gentle caress of the dawn, or feeling the breeze whip colour into your cheeks, are wholesome joys that can prepare you to face whatever else the rest of the day has in store.

Once you learn to notice and appreciate the free gifts that all of us keep receiving, once you grasp the skill of monitoring yourself in this fashion, you begin to see that everything that happens, every bit of information that comes your way, every big or small person who crosses your path, every victory or so-called 'defeat', has a message for you... provided you have the eyes to see, the ears to listen, and the sensibility to use what you thus register to its greatest possible advantage. For instance, I found to my delight, that many people (including those who matter) remembered me for the good work I had done. The exposure and recognition I had received, along with the innumerable worldwide contacts I had made during my tenure as police chief, came in handy when I set up my own office.

Of course the first few years were tough, but that is part and parcel of learning any new game. If my business had failed I would have been hard hit, because the pension a police job gives you is certainly not enough to keep you in style, or in any way afford you the perks you take for granted during your salad days in the force. You may help scores of people on-the-job, you may save hundreds of lives during a riot or any other social calamity, but the post-retirement compensation in no way matches your long years of commitment. Thankfully, my new enterprise turned the corner within a year, and now the key people in my team get more than what I earned at the peak of my career. That really feels good. Nurturing a project and watching it flourish is a joy money cannot buy.

Today, if some of the largest multinationals of the world consider my company a reliable agent to safeguard their interests and prevent infringement of their copyright or misuse of their trademark, it is because of the credibility created by my years in service. And therein lies a lesson: every seed sown with care and watched over with total diligence and love, without any thought of the rewards it will fetch, carries within it the potential of a golden harvest. It is not for nothing that the oft-quoted adage, 'Take care of today and tomorrow will take care of itself' has withstood the test of time.

The best spin-off of my 'years after' has been the fact that now I am the master of my own time. I work or shirk at will. I replace a day full of interminable meetings or surprise raids with a leisurely breakfast peppered with a cryptic crossword. A business tour is spiced-up with an exciting detour to watch an international cricket match, live!

During my years in the force, when I had to travel for twenty to twenty-five days of the month inspecting police cells of the district under my charge, I missed out on some vital stages in the growth of my children. The pain of that irreparable loss is soothed today by the rollicking times I have with my grandson. For now I can afford to distribute my workload in a manner that ensures that I can be with him during the hours that he is both free and at his most active.

Whenever a highly qualified individual in a top position is made to step down unceremoniously for the wrong reasons, he should remind himself repeatedly that it was his IQ and potential that had put him there in the first place. So if it helped him once, it can help him yet again to look for another job with a cleaner set-up, to diversify into another area of interest, to set up an independent venture like I did, or even to take a much-needed sabbatical. This helps clear the mind and waning self-confidence to re-surface, after which, what you do may well turn out to be a milestone move!

When your personal sky is overcast, when nothing seems to be going right, one temptation which proves to be a bad friend is the urge to complain about the unfairness of life. Not only does this fruitless exercise sap precious energy, it even dims your initiative to do something about your dilemma.

Besides, do people really listen to you when you grumble? They just wait for the tiniest pause, so that they can immediately begin their own sob-story. Some even encourage you to keep sinking in that cesspool of negativity because it reassures them that dwelling in one's misery rather than looking for a way out, is okay.

I have seen quite a few specimens of such human flotsam, soaked in self-pity and waiting endlessly for someone else to wake up and return their floundering dignity to them. A 'by-passed' man keeps hoping for a miracle that will give him the promotion or push-up he is convinced he deserves, another retired 'big-shot' club-trots and pours out his woes into yet another fragile glass as he awaits that elusive governor's post, or anything else that will lift this burden of anonymity off his shoulders and help him hold his head high again. Now tell me, who can understand you, support you, and incite you to pick yourself up and step into the battleground of life once more? Only you can.

At the same time, it pays to remember that life is not just about zooming ahead non-stop in a frantic chase for that elusive sprite called success in the world outside. Life is also about sitting still now and then. This really helps to gather your forces, acknowledge your plus points and mend your minus ones, to become aware of the immense possibilities that lie within and without for you to explore and become a complete person. If you truly understand that change is the most real and dynamic principle of the life cycle, letting go of something that has outlived its use, or to which you can no longer contribute as much as you would like to, comes easy.

That is when giving up anything which meant a lot does not become tantamount to defeat. That is when surrendering to the force of circumstance or destiny becomes an act of strength. That is when the fear of the unknown melts away.

> *Surrender is the simple but profound wisdom of 'yielding to' rather than 'opposing' the flow of life. The only place where you can experience the flow of life is the now, so the surrender is to accept the present moment unconditionally and without reservation. It is to relinquish inner resistance to what 'is'.*
>
> Eckhart Tolle

Once you have learnt to flow with life in this manner rather than flapping against its inexorable waves, true abundance comes to you in ways that could be described as 'miracles'. Moreover, you become so firmly rooted, so sure that life will open yet another gate for you to explore, that no wayward wind, no storm can break you any more. Here on, there is only growth, no holding back, and certainly no deterioration.

Two months before I joined the Police Academy, when flirting with words and dreaming of becoming a celebrity writer, if someone had told me that I would soon step into the harsh world of arms and ammunition, criminals and terrorists for a long and fruitful innings, I would have told him he was out of his mind. Yet, once I stepped in the arena to fight a protracted and harsh battle against injustice,

I was able to deal with (and, if necessary, even kill) inhuman people who posed a threat to the common man with the same sense of purpose with which you down a man-eater, or a deadly viper who has strayed into human habitation.

Achievements like this fetched me the expected laurels, no doubt. But once again, destiny tossed up a new card, set the dice rolling in a new direction. At the peak of my 'high' over the many accolades I received, if anyone had predicted that I would quit five years before my time was up, I would have definitely laughed in his face. But that is exactly what I did. So you see there is a pattern, a plan beyond what our eyes can see, or mind can fathom. The secret lies in intelligently processing all the experience one has gathered, and then intuitively deciding when to protest and when to walk away gracefully, if the umpire lifts his finger. The secret lies in spotting the difference between what one has to accept without qualms, and what one can, and must try to change for the better.

I will not deny that the excitement of my days in harness is missing from my itinerary. No crowds, no incessant calls, no bouquets or brickbats, no time-table without pause, no thundering applause. But in the mellow after-glow of a life well spent, solitude becomes a close friend rather than a dreaded enemy. Today silence generates untrammelled peace, rather than insecurity or unease.

ENDNOTE

IGP A. A. Khan was both the bane of terrorists and gangsters and the hero of his devoted ATS team. A gun-toting police chief who led from the front, he was also the delight of pun-happy reporters who nicknamed him 'Ack-Ack' Khan. His ability to act at moment's notice and unwillingness to let red-tape or political games delay or deter him, made him both unforgettable and 'transferable' in the unwritten history of the Indian police force.

What makes his tenure significant is the fact that his name was not even mentioned in the Sri Krishna Report, which was commissioned especially to put on record the true story behind the communal riots of 1992. Further, in spite of the fact that 44 hardcore criminals had been slain by him, A. A. Khan was not indicted by any commission of inquiry. All of this was his befitting reply to those who suspected his motives or questioned his rare courage. To sum up in his own words, "I work to please my conscience, not my bosses."

The author may be contacted on
email: aftab_a_khan2702@yahoo.co.in

For further details, contact:
Yogi Impressions LLP
1711, Centre 1, World Trade Centre,
Cuffe Parade, Mumbai 400 005, India.

Fill in the Mailing List form on our website
and receive, via email, information on
books, authors, events and more.
Visit: www.yogiimpressions.com

Telephone: (022) 61541500, 61541541
E-mail: yogi@yogiimpressions.com

Join us on Facebook:
www.facebook.com/yogiimpressions